Pastoral Care to the Sick in Africa.

STUDIEN ZUR INTERKULTURELLEN GESCHICHTE DES CHRISTENTUMS
ETUDES D'HISTOIRE INTERCULTURELLE DU CHRISTIANISME
STUDIES IN THE INTERCULTURAL HISTORY OF CHRISTIANITY

begründet von/fondé par/founded by
Hans Jochen Margull †, Hamburg

herausgegeben von/édité par/edited by

Richard Friedli
Université de Fribourg

Walter J. Hollenweger
University of Birmingham

Theo Sundermeier
Universität Heidelberg

Jan A. B. Jongeneel
Rijksuniversiteit Utrecht

Band 51

Verlag Peter Lang
Frankfurt am Main · Bern · New York · Paris

Abraham Adu Berinyuu

PASTORAL CARE TO THE SICK IN AFRICA

An Approach to Transcultural Pastoral Theology

Verlag Peter Lang

Frankfurt am Main · Bern · New York · Paris

CIP-Titelaufnahme der Deutschen Bibliothek

Berinyuu, Abraham Adu:

Pastoral care to the Sick in Africa : an Approach to
Transcultural Pastoral Theology / Abraham Adu Berinyuu. -
Frankfurt am Main ; Bern ; New York ; Paris : Lang, 1988
(Studien zur interkulturellen Geschichte des Christentums ;
Bd. 51)
Zugl.: Atlantic School of Theology, Diss., 1987
ISBN 3-8204-1660-9

NE: GT

ISSN 0170-9240
ISBN 3-8204-1660-9

© Verlag Peter Lang GmbH, Frankfurt am Main 1988.

Printed in Germany

To my mother, Menvolima, a major source of inspiration; the late Rev. Dr. Jacob Jamani Natomah of Mimima in Northern Ghana whose friendship I will ever miss; and to all pastoral caregivers in Africa, Africans and foreign missionaries who in diverse ways heal the sick, comfort the mourning and the hurt, strengthen the weak and reconcile the estranged.

PREFACE

AFRICAN AND WESTERN MEDICINE IN DIALOGUE

Ghanaian Christians seem to be particularly interested in the contribution of traditional African healers (Berinyuu calls them "diviners") to health and welfare and especially to Christian pastoral care. Kofi Appiah-Kubi[1] and Emmanuel Yartekwei Lartey[2] are two researchers who have recently drawn attention to this important field, the former from a medical, the latter from a theological point of view.

In this work Abraham Adu Berinyuu asks the question: What is the appropriate pastoral approach in a society such as the Ghanaian, which, long before the arrival of the missionaries, had a flourishing tradition and a body of experts for dealing with the sick? How does a Christian "diviner", a Christian minister, approach this problem taking into account the pre-Christian traditions and insights of his ancestors and also the differences between a Christian and a non-Christian approach? Such a ministry "does not insist that Christian theology manufactured in some other cultural milieu should fit into an African situation, nor does it insist that Christian theology should give up its unique claims to African culture" (p. 91f.). In this field it becomes clearer than anywhere else that "Christian theology is universal only when it can be particular" (p. 92).

For Berinyuu, to be particular means for example that a Christian minister/priest in Africa can justifiably be called a diviner. "In fact, the word Osofo in Akan applied to the Christian ministers, connotes a form of divination" (p. 93). "The christian diviner therefore has a task of relating the language of the pain expressed through the symbols of the church to that of the good news of Christ Jesus" (p. 93f.). For him "the patient is not a disease entity or medical problem to be treated with surgery, radiation or chemotherapy, healing is a process of profound dimensions, involving virtually all aspects of a person's life - physical, spiritual, psychological, social dimensions, environmental and even political."[3] The process, the relationship between diviner and patient is more important than the treatment prescribed. Because the Christian diviner is a "listener of stories" the patient can tell the diviner/minister his/her story and thus understand and re-interpret it.

The christological implications Berinyuu draws from such an indigenised form of pastoral care, are interesting and important. Jesus can be seen in an African society as "a first ancestor" (John 1.1). Patients are "ready to believe because a first ancestor, Jesus, died to free them, heal them and accept them at death into the community of saints" (p. 103).

The Christian diviner will make clear that salvation "only means that one's life in health and in sickness, in hope and in doubts, in joys and in sorrows is mediated through Christ so that one can participate in the love of God, which gives meaning to all existence. It does not guarantee problem-proof and sickness-free life." (p. 104). Hence the difference between a Christian and a pre-Christian diviner.

In practical terms Berinyuu sees the rite of anointing with oil as a means by which this is not only declared but experienced. This is a very interesting development because Swiss and other Reformed/Presbyterian churches have come to the same conclusions. There is no question of giving up the centrality of the theology of the cross. But what is the good of such a theology if it fails at the test-bed, in sickness and trial? It is surely not good enough just to preach it. It has to be felt, experienced and ritually internalised.[4]

Anointing with oil can heal or strengthen or prepare for the great and difficult journey into death. Which one it will be is not in our hands.

European mission societies and the World Health Organisation in Geneva begin to realise too that our contribution to African health can no longer be that of exporting our medical technology and rejecting African medicine as superstition. It is both in the interests of Western medicine and theology and of the African churches and societies to initiate an informed dialogue. For such a dialogue, this book is a good and helpful start.

Dr. Walter J. Hollenweger
Professor of Mission
University of Birmingham

Footnotes

[1]Kofi Appiah-Kubi, Man Cures, God Heals. Religion and Medical Practice Among the Akans of Ghana (New York: Friendship Press, 1981). See also from a Western point of view: Beatrix Pfleiderer/Wolfgang Bichmann, Krankheit and Kultur. Eine Einführung in die Ethnodmedizin (Berlin, Dietrich Reimer Verlag, 1985).

[2]E.Y. Lartey, Pastoral Counselling in Inter-Cultural Perspective. A study of some African (Ghanaian) and Anglo-American views on human existence and counselling (in this series, vol. 43, Frankfurt/Berne/New York, Peter Lang, 1987).

[3]Richard Yadeau, "Healing", World and War 11 (4) (Fall 1982): 319; quoted in Berinyuu, p. 94.

[4]This and other points mentioned in this preface are discussed in detail and amply documented in W.J. Hollen-weger, Geist und Materie. Interkulturelle Theologie III (Munich: Kaiser, 1988).

ACKNOWLEDGEMENTS

This book is written with all pastoral caregivers in mind, but specifically for those in Africa. My attempt here is to join the discussion and the struggle of making the christian ministry of healing relevant in Africa.

Having lived, ministered in, and experienced the complex nature of ministry in Africa, I hope that this book invokes anger and determination in others to develop better opinions to make ministry authentic to African christians and also to add a perspective to the christian church worldwide.

Hence, if this book stimulates others to question more and seek earnestly for an authentic African christian approach it will have achieved its aim.

I am eternally indebted to all who have enabled me in diverse ways. It is practically impossible to list all of their names, so it is neither forgetfulness nor ingratitude that your name is not listed. The best I can do is to put you in groupings: personal friends, teachers, and pasters. My wife, Esther Afisah derverves special thanks. She has not only supported me but taught me a lot by being who she is.

I must, however, mention those who have made a direct contribution to this volume. I thank Dr. W.T. Hollenweger, a Professor of Mission in the University of Birmingham. He painstakingly read through the script and made valuable suggestions. He made the publishing of this book possible.

I also thank Dr. Jacques Goulet, Professor at Mount St. Vincent University, Halifax, Nova Scotia. He was my pastor and guide at the beginning of this project.

My thanks and gratitude to Dr. James Lapsley Jr., Dr. Don Capps and Dr. Geddes Hanson, all of Princeton Theological Seminary, who have also given me valuable help.

This project would not have been possible without the financial support of Knox College, Toronto, the Gordon Fellowship of the United Church of Canada, and the Dr. Arthur Betts Fellowship at the Atlantic School of Theology, Halifax, Nova Scotia.

My thanks also to the Presbyterian Church of Ghana for its nurture and permission to pursue further studies.

All said and done, I accept full responsibility for all opinions expressed in this book.

Abraham Adu Berinyuu

XI

TABLE OF CONTENTS

1. INTRODUCTION

The christian church via the western missionary enter-
prise has been in Africa since the fifteenth century. As
the church expanded in mission, so it also expanded in
ministry. At times, one was used as a vehicle of the other. The christian church as part of its ministry of healing brought hospitals to many parts of Africa. This ministry of healing, by way of hospitals and clinics in rural
areas, has tremendously reduced infant mortality, and has
also increased the average span of life of most Africans.
The debatable question is whether the hospitals were introduced to help reduce or even eliminate African 'suspicions'
of illness, or as vehicles of God's healing love. I do not
intend to pursue this dabatable question in detail here,
nonetheless, it does relate wholly or partially to the
western mission churches' practice of the healing ministry
of the church to the sick.

The ministry or model of pastoral care presently practiced by most mission churches' christians, both lay and
ordained, will be briefly described. The immediate response of a pastoral care giver to any church member who
complains of some sickness is, "Go to the hospital", or
"Have you gone to the hospital?"

It is this author's suspicion that some Africans approach the western trained doctor with an African notion of
the "witch doctor" who diagnoses both physical and spiri-

tual illness at one and the same time. Thus, in that kind of instant referral, many of the clergy and others in pastoral care (as well-intended and perhaps ultimately helpful as the referral may be), may be abdicating their role to some extent. It is the aim of this author to explore ways of enhancing the therapeutic role of native culture, and the rich dimension which that culture can contribute to the church's ministry of healing to their followers who become sick.

The primary purpose here is a formulation of some valid approaches of christian pastoral care to christians who fall sick. In this approach, the model of dialectic dialogue of christian theology and the psycho-social and spiritual dimension of treatment to the sick in African culture will be given attention. It is not trying to make christian theology fit into the African category of things, neither is it shaping African categories of things to fit into christian theology. Mutual respect and honesty are important criteria in this model of dialectical dialogue.

The goal in this understanding is to provide a transcultural approach that will enrich the overall understanding of the christian ministry of healing to the sick in Africa. It is a search for an authentic christian theology of pastoral care that is neither patronizing or paternalistic for both parties involved. It does not seek to resolve the differences, rather it aims at using them to enhance the christian ministry of pastoral care.

This attempt at a transcultural christian theology of pastoral care is an effort to make the "word of God" incarnate in the people of God in Africa. For the christian ministry of healing to be relevant, calls for an unorthodox approach. It is presenting Christ in a relevant, contextual and meaningful way to the christians in their African situation. It is an attempt to translate the gospel of Jesus Christ into African languages, thought forms, concepts and praxis. For Africans to believe and live with Jesus as Lord, especially in times of sickness, does not mean they should be turned into Europeans, Asians or Americans. Instead, Jesus comes and enters deeply into the holistic African world view and ethos. This approach attempts to make the salvation of the cross of Jesus, the Christ into a wholeness of life which includes, holistic healing; body, soul and spirit, social redemption and reconciliation.

It is therefore, imperative that our starting point is not western psychology or philosophy, not even western christian theology of pastoral care. It is not that western psychology, philosophy, and even theology of pastoral care cannot and may not be useful and appropriate; it is in some cases. But our laboratory must be Africa and our specimen Africans. Our conclusions can only be valid, appropriate and valuable in their intent and content when

We start with Africa and Africans therein. Hence, in this book, the African ethos and world view, concept of person, sickness and approaches to healing are paramount.

I. Therefore, I proceed with the following pastoral theological assumptions: a) that God has not left himself/herself without a witness among all peoples of the earth; b) that the spirit of God is actively present in what all people do to cope in times of crisis or in their understanding of some of the mysteries of life; and c) that these mechanisms of coping and/or of trying to understand the mysteries of life are worth sharing with the rest of God's people and must of necessity be incorporated into the gospel of Jesus Christ in order to make the gospel meaningful, freeing, and enriching the quality of relationships among all people.

In this book, the terms sickness and illness are used interchangeably to connote the same effect in the victim, notwithstanding the differences in opinion about sickness, disease and illness. The focus of this approach to healing is on the psycho-social and ritualistic aspects. The soma-physical treatment is linked with the medical or herbal and so it is not given attention. The theological frame of this thesis is reformed bias. However, in suggesting an approach, it is the meaning of sickness in African culture, and the witness of scripture that become the determining factors.

2. THE ETHOS AND WORLD VIEW OF AFRICANS

As an introduction to the chapter, the words ethos and world view will be defined. Clifford Geertz offers a definition most appropriate for this thesis. According to Geertz,

> A people's ethos is the tone, character and quality of their life, its moral and aesthetic style and mood. It is the underlying attitude towards themselves and their world in that life reflects. Their world view is their picture of the way things in sheer actuality are, their concept of nature, of self, of society.[1]

Of the many definitions and usages of these terms, those offered by Geertz reflect most African communities, hence are appropriate working definitions for this book.

In this chapter the traditional world view of black Africans and the relationship of a person to the community will be described. The discussion will dwell chiefly on the psycho-social or psycho-cultural, and spiritual aspects of African world view and a person.

World View

In Africa, there is no division and/or differentiation between the animate and inanimate, between spirit and matter, between living and non-living, dead and living, physical and metaphysical, secular and sacred, the body and spirit, etc. Most Africans generally believe that everything (human beings included) is in constant relationship with one another and with the invisible world, and that people are in a state of complete dependence upon those invisible powers and beings. Hence, Africans are convinced that in the activities of life, harmony, balance or tranquility must constantly be sought and maintained. Society is not segmented into, for example, medicine, sociology, law, politics, and religion. Life is a liturgy of celebration for the victories and/or sacrifices of others.

Kofi Appiah-Kubi in his social survey of the Akans, brings out this concept clearly when he writes,

> The Akans seek the welfare of the community and the lineage, for the clan is the basis of the social and political and moral obligations. The custodians of such morality are not only the ancestors but the whole of the spirit world, including the gods.[2]

Societies may be divided into clans and even into tribal units but nonetheless Africans view their world as an integrated one. This point is further supported in a report on his research among the Tallensis of Ghana by Meyer Fortes. He concludes:

> The clans belonging to each group are more closely interlinked by clanship and politico- ritual ties. [The clans] have very close bonds of local contiguity, and of politico-ritual interdependence and cooperation in assuring the maintenance of the common interests of the society -- peace and the rule of custom, fertility of soil and of man [bearing children] and prosperity.[3]

The human person is not an isolated individual in this world view. He/she is at all times interacting with other beings in the universe, whom he/she is linked to by a network of relationships. The human being is essentially a member of a community of beings as well as a unique indi-

vidual person. He/she is a force in a universe of living

forces, a member of the community of humans, while at the

same time, a unique individual endowed with the responsi-

bility to create and share life in the universe.

The world view of the Africans can be likened to a

Rubik Cube. All the sides and colours of the sides form an

integrated, patterned whole. If one side, or a set of

sides and colours shift, the whole Rubik Cube is in dis-

array. For the Rubik Cube to be in order, every side,

every colour and every cube must be in its proper place.

Shift one and you upset the unity of the design; bring it

back into position and the entire Rubik Cube is restored

wholly. Similarly in Africa, if someone breaks the moral

rules of community, this simultaneously disturbs the cosmic

ties between the person and the community, thus

> prefiguring a wide social disturbance spreading
> from the individual kinship, [clan] and immediate
> wife and children. But the disorder may be cor-
> rected by the appropriate rituals which restore
> the individual general order.[4]

Any discussion of the traditional African world view

would be incomplete without the mention of the ancestors.

What Mercy Amba Oduyoye describes as the role of ancestors

among black Africans in general is true. She writes that

> the role of the ancestors in the life of Africans
> becomes important in enabling them to remember
> their source and history. To deny history is to
> deny one's roots and source of self-identity. It
> is also to deny the fact that we embody in our-
> selves both the past, present and future.[5]

Africans believe that the ancestors have become pro-
tectors of their lives and society. For this reason, among
both the Akans and the Tallensis, before the elderly eat,
they first throw a morsel of food on the ground. Before
they drink water, which is the traditional symbol of wel-
come to every visitor, they pour some on the floor, thus
giving water to the spirits of the ancestors who accompany
the living in daily errands. Ancestors have such a tremendous influence on the daily life of most Africans that
western anthropologists and theologians wrongly supposed
that they are worshipped. Africans do believe strongly in
the presence and influence of ancestors in daily life, so
much so that they do things, often unconsciously, to reflect such a belief but they do not worship them as gods.
Alyward Shorter illustrates this clearly when he writes,

> People bear the names of their ancestors. The
> bearers of the names are thought to have a very
> close relationship to their namesakes.[6]

John Pobee's observation of a Methodist clergyman further
substantiates this point. According to John Pobee, this
minister had been strongly attacking the practice of pour-
ing libation, a practice whereby black Africans evoke the
spirits of the dead and offer them drink and food. John
Pobee observed that, before this Methodist minister (who
opposed libation as pagan) drank, he would pour some of the
drink on the floor. John Pobee later asked him why he did
that. The minister replied, "because a fly was in the

glass."[7] John Pobee draws his conclusion:

> True; houseflies are a humbug in tropical Africa.
> But the consistency with which the pouring of the
> drink was done, always before a drink, morning,
> afternoon, evening and night, made me believe
> [the minister's explanation] was a clever after-
> the-fact rationalization of a world taken-for-
> granted, which is just beneath the surface, so to
> speak, and which surfaces when the chips are
> down.[8]

John Pobee's analysis of the Ghanaian practices is

common in most communities in Africa. He writes,

> Behind all such acts, at both the individual and
> communal levels, stands the rationale that a
> person is surrounded by numerous host of spirit-
> beings, some good, some evil which can and do
> influence the course of human life for good or
> for ill. Consequently, their goodwill is active-
> ly and constantly sought, thereby acknowledging
> the dependence of the living on the spirit
> world.[9]

John Pobee's summary of religion vis-a-vis the Ghana world

view is similar for most communities in Africa.

> Religion is all-pervasive in Akan society
> [Ghanaian society]. Thus a good deal of the
> communal activities of the Akan and other social
> institutions are inextricably bound up with reli-
> gion and the spirit world. Birth, puberty, mar-
> riage, death, widowhood, harvest, and instal-
> lations to traditional offices all partake a
> religious nature.[10]

John Pobee continues his analysis:

> Apart from God, the ancestor's and the gods'
> nature is believed to have power and even spir-
> its. Behind the offering [of drink and/or food]
> stands their theory of reality: [that] behind
> the visible substance of things lies essences or
> powers which constitute their true nature. Na-
> ture has power which may be reversed as well as
> harnessed to man's benefit. Religion is tradi-
> tionally the most important sphere of cultural
> activity that nursed the health of a nation.[11]

In both of the foregoing and what follows, the astute
western reader may note some resemblance to the emerging
world picture being pieced together in the western science
of ecology.

Person and Community

Human beings are an integral part of the world view
described above. They are not principal partners, but
minor partners in this cosmology. Some examples from the
Akans and the Tallensis will illustrate this point.

Among the Akans, a person's <u>Kra</u> is the life energy
which connects him/her to God. The <u>ntroro</u> spirit is the
energy which links him/her to the ancestral lineage. Meyer
Fortes' extensive research and writings on the Tallensis
reveal that among the Tallensis

> one's bond with one's lineage implies a ritual
> bond with one's patrilineal ancestors and other
> mystical forces associated with the existence and
> well being of the lineage. They [ancestral spir-
> its and other spiritual beings/forces] are the
> chief mystical powers governing the life of the
> individual.[12]

Meyer Fortes continues his analysis that "the ancestor
spirits are the principal sanction enforcing a man's right
to full filial status in his physical lineage".[13]

The Ghanaians, like other communities such as the
Dogon,

> think of a person as participating in the general
> condition of his society and the universe. A
> newly born child is only potentially a human
> being and must be given his own sexual, social

and spiritual identity by the human community
into which he is born.[14]

Benjamin Ray adopts the term "destiny" from Fortes and

tries to make psychological comparisons which in the writ-

er's opinion only confuse and trivialize a very highly

religious dimension of a person among the Tallensis. He

writes:

> as Fortes has pointed out, the Tale view of man
> rests upon notions of fate and responsibility
> which are comparable to classical western formu-
> lations--for example, the stories of Oedipus and
> Job.[15]

One is of the impression that "Fate" is derived from what

Fortes calls destiny which is his translation of the Tallen

word yin. Among the Tallensis, before a person is born or

shorty thereafter, the parent consults a diviner to know

who is his/her yin, translated by Fortes as destiny. Yin

in Tallen is the guarding and guiding spirit of the child,

and is usually one of the ancestors. Benjamin Ray con-

tinues:

> each youth finds himself chosen by a specific
> [one] or group of guardian ancestors who will
> preserve and give his life beyond the stage gov-
> erned by his infantile and dangerous prenatal
> destiny.[16]

Benjamin Ray makes an incorrect analysis when he

writes:

> the first is a fatalistic and amoral vision; the
> second [I suppose he is referring to adulthood]
> is freedom--affirming and supremely moral. But
> whereas in western thought these two visions [I
> suppose he is referring to prenatal to teen and
> youth to adult] of a man are unconditionally
> opposed; in Tale thought; they were dynamically

combined as two related phases in man's socio-religious development. Men move beyond the infantile, presocial sphere of destiny [Oedipus fate] into the realm of moral responsibility before the ancestors [Job and God]. The Tallensis project a dynamic vision of man [personhood]; he is both fated and free, innocent and responsible, Oedipus and Job.[17]

Benjamin Ray gives the impression of a concept of progress from fatalism to responsibility. He comes to this conclusion because of his wrong translation of yin, a guarding ancestral spirit, as destiny, and then constructs and imposes a psychology of development on the Tallensis. The fact is that one's yin (guarding and guiding spirit of one of the ancestors of one's clan) is chosen before, at, or shortly after, birth, and there are elaborate rituals accompanying the occasion. Indeed, throughout the days of one's life, one's yin becomes the focus in success, failure, sickness, in health and in death and even after death. What Ray fails to understand is that before and at birth up to teenage, one's parent exercises the rituals, sacrifices, etc., on one's behalf. At adulthood, the individual has a direct personal responsibility of seeking the protection and blessing of one's yin on him/her. However, Benjamin Ray makes an interesting analysis with the aid of Robin Horton.

Robin Horton is quoted as having compared the notion of yin, which he also translates "destiny", with the western concept of the unconscious. Benjamin Ray writes quoting Robin Horton:

> fundamentally to both [destiny and unconscious]
> concepts is the notion that a successful life
> requires the 'acceptance' of factors stemming
> essentially from within the self. In this con-
> cept, the African concept of personal destiny is
> not analogous to the Greek concept of an arbi-
> trary impersonal and unalterable fate. Rather,
> like the idea of the unconscious, destiny is
> understood to be a hidden but determinative part
> of the self which is both controllable and uncon-
> trollable to the extent that it is revealed to
> the individual and accepted by him. As part of
> the personality 'chosen' before birth, destiny is
> only gradually disclosed to the individual in a
> series of traumatic situations. But once it is
> revealed it can be partially modified, as can the
> hidden desires and conflicts imposed by the un-
> conscious. In this way a person may better ad-
> just to the circumstances of his society and to
> the exigencies of life.[18]

This analysis is very helpful in a discussion of sickness

and has interesting parallels with the concept of an indi-

vidual's having a personal "myth". While the efforts of

Robin Horton and Benjamin Ray are admirable in attempting

to understand African personality through western psychol-

ogy, their attempt to reduce the African personality to fit

western psychological categories denies African ideas of

personality as personhood to stand on their own and be

treated with respect and dignity.

To understand how most Africans perceive a person one

must realize that there is no direct connection between the

christian concept of God and individual among Ghanaians.

In most African communities, there are myths of how God

physically withdrew from the physical earth. Some myths

suggest it was because the sky (some African dialects use sky for God) was burnt, or a rope was broken. The genesis notion of creation and fall may be similar but, most Africans hardly trace their history or life of the ancestors once in paradise. The sense of the fall is also foreign to most Africans. That does not, however, mean that Africans do not believe in God or that God has no part in the make-up of a person. Africans do believe in a personal element that cannot be destroyed by any evil spirit or by death. What it is called and how it is accounted for is outside the scope of this book. However, Africans do strongly believe that God uses ancestors and other spiritual beings as agents of blessing and cursing. In addition, there are certainly evil spirits allowed occasionally to affect an individual. These evil spirits are by their nature and origin evil. Here again, their source is not clearly articulated. God can and does use the ancestors, allows even the evil spirits, but is beyond all and can overrule all. Africans also believe that human beings need to depend on the ancestors, now spirits, to plead with God on their behalf, because God is spirit and only spirit can communicate with spirit. The activities of God are not limited however to the spirits of the ancestors. In his book, I. Sow makes some general observations of the African perception of God. He writes:

In Africa, man [person] is permeated with a world
that is crowded, strudded with a myriad of signi-
fiers, visible and invisible, penetrating every
facet of life. This world is dominated by the
presence of a supreme being, a universal ruler
presiding over the destinies of humans, animals,
plants, things. Eternal and omniscient God the
creator is at the center of existence even though
he has withdrawn [physically invisible] from the
world of humans, can make himself manifest on the
earth, in the air, or in the water at any time,
in the most diverse forms. He is a hidden force,
an imperceptible energy that diffuses throughout
the whole expanse of the cosmos, determining the
cycle of seasons, the movement of the stars, the
activities of the four great natural elements
[rain, wind, vegetation and lightning].[19] In
short, his power and dominion is boundless.

I. Sow also makes a valuable observation which is very

relevant to note. He observes that

it is impossible to think of African psychology
and à fortiori, African psychopathology without
reference to the anthropological structures of
the self in the various stages of traditional
life.[20]

Again he expresses what is very true of Africans thus:

there is no doubt that African thought has a
distinctive character, deriving its principles
from symbols and myths [merging into one the
universe and the society in which the African
person/personality is formed] as well as from a
collective ritual permitting precise location of
the individual in relation to his environment and
to the course of his development.[21]

Of the different schools of thought in personology, I

believe the so called folk tradition theory throws more

light on the concept of a person in Africa.

The folk tradition is best understood from the per-

spective of biology and anthropology. In folk tradition:

life is a convenient source of psychological
information. Through folk tradition humans learn
how and in what ways all people are different and
provide a means for explaining particular enigmatic and puzzling actions.[22]

This approach is common in almost all primary societies.

It is certainly true for Ghanaians. This is the emic (view

from the inside out) perspective, to borrow a helpful meta-

phor used by Schreiter.

One major criticism of the emic perspective which is

valid in this discussion is well articulated by Robert

Schreiter in his discussion of "the description and per-

spective in culture."[23] Robert Schreiter writes:

> From the inner perspective, the description will
> often be characterized by narrative. Explanation
> may occur, but usually to support the narrative
> rather than to translate it into another mode of
> discourse. Thus in describing marriage patterns,
> someone from the inside might begin by talking
> about who has married whom. Explanations will
> remain internal to the system. It is meant to
> reaffirm realities rather than dissect them.
> Good description is judged by how well it rein-
> forces the identity of those on the inside.[24]

Two German words that mean personality in English are

personlichkeit and personalitat. The definitions of Robert

Hogan are helpful, hence adopted here.

> Personlichkeit refers to the distinctive impres-
> sion that a person makes on others. The root of
> the word personality is the latin term persona,
> the mask worn by an actor to signify a role in a
> play. This form of personality is tied to a
> contrived public appearance, personality in this
> sense is a function of the immediate social sit-
> uation. It suggests uniqueness in style and
> superficiality in commitment.

> Personality in the sense of personalitat refers
> to the fundamental core of man [and woman], to

the essential person that lives at the center of
our being. Personality in this sense refers to
the deep, enduring and often innate structures
within a person whose existence, typically, can
only be inferred. Because of its innate properties, personality in this second sense is usually
seen as autonomous and unchanging.[25]

Personality as personlitat contrasted with the Ghana-

ian view of a person shows some strong differences. The

first difference is that Ghanaians, and indeed most Afric-

ans, believe that a person is not a finished product. The

concept of personality as personalitat does suggest the

contrary. Another difference resulting from the difference

just stated is that the Ghanaian concept of personality has

a lot of input from society, whereas the personalitat con-

cept downplays, if not denies, the influence of society.

There however is one similarity. Both do agree that per-

sonality has some innate structures and properties. The

Ghanaian view of a person's innate qualities may come from

the spirits of the ancestors, while the concept of person-

alitat may be traced to genes or what Robert Hogan called

"biogenics". I believe that beyond semantics, there is a

commonality in these two concepts.

In the etymology of personality as personlichkeit

referred to earlier, the word "mask" suggests something

negative, fictitious, unreal, or even the notion of mimick-

ing. However, Carl Jung who makes use of the notion of a

mask, draws a meaning which is similar to the Ghanaian

notion of a person. According to Jung,

> The persona is only a mask for the collective psyche, a mask that feigns individuality and tries to make others and oneself believe that one is individual, whereas one is simply playing a part in which the collective psyche speaks.[26]

The Ghanaian concept of a person partially acts according to the norms of society. This notion of role is similar to the meaning given by George Kelly, a leading scholar in the field of personality. For him,

> a role is a pattern of behavior that follows from one's perception of what another person expects of him [her].[27]

This meaning of role is different from its usage by some sociologists, for some sociologists

> a role is a pattern of behaviour that is associated with a particular social position, and anyone who occupies that position should behave accordingly.[28]

Most anthropologists and sociologists writing on African concepts of person tend to make such associations. There is something basic missing in these two assessments of role vis-a-vis African perceptions of a person and the role of that person. Both definitions leave out a central element of conviction. Roles of Africans are not like wearing an already made shirt or hat. For Africans, it is not something only imposed upon by an outside agent. The "buyer" is part of the material that is woven into the hat or the shirt. In the process of weaving, there arises a _conviction_ and hence an identity with the material used for weaving, the processing or weaving and the finished product, namely the hat or shirt. Africans are aware, consciously or unconsciously, of other influences on human beings as materials in the process of weaving and in the finished product. This is illustrated in the belief that behind every human being is a spiritual guardian who caused the beginning of his/her life and has been actively protecting and guiding him/her. This spirit, the Tallensis refer to as the yin which can also be translated "god", either with a small 'g' or a capital 'G', or the equivalent of the notion of a guardian angel in Roman Catholicism.

The west has had a long history of dividing a person into matter and spirit. For Africans, "life and the person are of a spiritual order."[29] Though psychology is important and helpful in understanding a person, and though medicine is helpful and necessary to heal a person, the spiritual dimension of a person is the most important aspect of the self and of psychological health. The spiritual dimension of a person is all important. Despite the abuse, misuse, and underuse of religion in interpreting and helping a person in sickness, the religious dimension is vital for an African understanding of a person and should consequently be given serious attention in health, in sickness, and more importantly, in the treatment of illness. An analogy from Paul Tournier is helpful here:

> There are in an orchestra two big principal groups of instruments, strings and wind. We may compare them to the two constituent elements of the living being, the body and the mind. The invisible conductor of the orchestra controls

both these groups of instruments at the same time and co-ordinates them. He makes a sign first to the one and then to the other to take up the principal theme, in accordance with the plan laid down by the composer.[36]

Like all analogies, this one has its weaknesses, but it does make a point. In this analogy, the body is the physiological, the mind is the psyche, and the conductor is the spiritual dimension, the spiritual dimension may be put in theological terms as the Imago Dei. The composer is God, the Creator, although admittedly, the influence of God on the whole person is much broader and deeper than that of a composer on the orchestra. In the individual's "orchestra", all the elements are needed to produce beautiful smooth music.

Put in theological language, salvation must be affected by and through the body, the wind, the conductor and the composer. Paul Tournier seems to echo this view when he says,

> it is neither the body which controls the mind, nor the mind which controls the body, rather both are at once the expression of an invisible reality of a spiritual order--the person[31]

This view of a person agrees with the African view of a person. Paul Tournier expresses this eloquently when he concludes that:

> Such a conception of man is infinitely more satisfying to the mind than a purely organic or a purely psychogenic conception, or again one that is alternatively organicist and psychogenic. According to it [the holistic approach] it is a spiritual impulsion, man's spiritual destiny,

which controls both his [her] bodily and his
mental phenomena, whether normal or pathological.
The body and mind are only the means of expres-
sion of the Spirit[32]which coordinates and directs
them both at once.

Two medical cases cited by Paul Tournier offer evi-

dence. A specialist in tuberculosis in Norway who con-

ducted a psychological study of some tuberculosis patients

has shown that the evolutive phases of the disease regularly coincide with periods during which
the mind is troubled by serious inner conflicts,
particularly moral conflicts.[33]

The conclusion of Paul Tournier is that a serious conflict

of conscience is not merely a psychological fact, it is an

intimate spiritual event which expresses itself in two ways

at once--in the physical manifestations which

Dr. Huebschmann [the specialist] studies by means
of analysis and in the physical symptoms revealed
by auscultation and radiography.[34]

The second case concerns a woman who also suffered

from tuberculosis. The woman was a Roman Catholic who

married for a second time to a Protestant, once married

There were conflicts concerning the children of
her husband's first marriage. But soon, she
opened her heart more deeply. During adoles-
cence, while in a Catholic boarding school, she
had formed an association with a schoolmate from
abroad who was passionately addicted to the read-
ing of Nietzsche. She herself was still immature
mentally, incapable of holding her own argument
with a stronger mind. She was convinced that the
religion she had been taught was nothing but an
illusion. Thereafter, she even found it impossible at the time of the tragic death of her
first husband. She felt that she lacked something, but had never found anyone to whom she
could talk about it. Following our conversation,
she found her Catholic faith again. From that

time the condition of her lungs rapidly improved.
Four months later, my colleague [the specialist]
was able to announce that she was cured of tuberculosis.[35]

While this case may be considered as an isolated case,

nevertheless,

> This case is a good illustration of this funda-
> mental problem of relationship to soul, mind and
> body. There existed a spiritual problem which
> was comprised of at the same time both her physi-
> cal and her mental health, with the result that
> my colleague found physical symptoms and I found
> physical symptoms. The recounting of life story,
> a mind thinking aloud, freed from the bonds of
> formalism, leads one inevitably to the consider-
> ation of problems, such as the meaning of life
> and of the world, of disease and of death, of sin
> and of faith, or one's own scale of values.[36]

From the African view of personality, together with

the western view implicit in the two cases cited, it seems

safe and valid to conclude with the words of Paul Tournier

that:

> Life, the spirit, the person are not substantial
> realities which we can hold in our hands. They
> cannot be docketed, analysed, or described. They
> are as fleeting as a lightning flash--by the time
> we have seen their light and heard the rumbling
> that follows them, they have already gone. We
> cannot reach the person either by means of intro-
> spection or by objective scientific study alone.
> Let us now, therefore seek another way of ap-
> proach.[37]

Finally, the discussion of a person can be related to

the Biblical understanding of person and community. The

Biblical view of person, like the traditional Ghanaian

view, is primarily a religious one. The Bible does not

minimize the materials which were used to create human

beings, but it must be emphasized that the main focus in these stories (Gen. 1:27, Gen. 2:7) is the Imago Dei. Psychology, as we know it now, was not of any interest in the Biblical understanding of a person, although it was not altogether absent.

In the Old Testament, there are two notions of a person which reflect two periods of history. There is

> One prior to the prophets, a period of collectivism in which the protest of the individual conscience makes itself heard against Social Conformity, the protest of Justice against routine.[38]

For the people of Israel, their identity as a people was based on their theological experience of election and covenant, starting from Abraham to the exodus, and indeed throughout their history. Their religious experience controlled their organic identity--Communitas ac societas unitae. Consequently,

> in the very functioning of this collective responsibility the particular dignity of man [woman] is manifest. The whole family of Achan is destroyed because of the fault of one (Josh. 7:24). The iniquity of the fathers is visited upon the sons (Exo. 20:5). There is even solidarity reward: the righteous of Noah saves his whole family (Gen. 7:1). The house of Obed Edom is blessed because he has given shelter to the Ark (2 Sam. 6:11).[39]

In the above statement, the individual plays a vital role with respect to the functioning and/or fate of the community. Roger Mehl drives this point home when he says,

> because an individual has the power of being a blessing or a curse to the whole people, the individual is not without value in the eyes of God.[40]

It is from this particular understanding that the term

"corporate personality" is derived; defined as

> the whole group, composed of past and future
> members, [which] can act as a single individual
> in and through the activity of any member what-
> soever[41] conceived as a representative of the
> group.

The absence of the present, which is very important in the

Ghanaian view of corporate personality, weakens this defin-

ition.

Notwithstanding the absence of the present, Roger's

view echoes the sentiments of the African traditional no-

tion of corporate personality, and it is worth noting that

this sense of corporate personality in Israel is supported

by Biblical evidence. For example

> Adam and Israel are presented to us as at the
> same time both individual persons and as types
> representing a whole race of people. In the same
> way, the 'I' of the psalms and the whole nation,
> and the servant of the eternal is an ambivalent
> being, representing both a person and the people
> of Israel.[42]

Roger Mehl concludes that

> The individual is therefore never conceived [of]
> as a separate being, enclosed in his own soli-
> tude, a kind of atom [an unfortunate western
> tendency]. He is always thought of in solidarity
> with his people, and with his ancestral line.
> Apart from this solidarity, he would have no
> authentic existence, not being a beneficiary of
> the promise and of the covenant. But this soli-
> darity is not mechanical. It finds expression in
> a consciousness of personal responsibility.[43]

The parallels of Mehl's Biblical understanding of community

and person, and the traditional African view stated ear-

lier, are too close.

Person and community as presented in the New Testament, illustrates that the traditional Ghanaian view and
the christian witness today, generally speaking, are not
that different from each other. In the New Testament the
early christian community gathered around the resurrected
Christ. By faith and baptism, they had entered the Church
of God by confession of Jesus as the Christ. The author of
the letter of Romans (especially 6:3-11) emphasizes that by
baptism, christians participate in the life, death and
resurrection of Christ Jesus. Baptism initiates them into
the union with God, hence they share in the mission of
Jesus Christ in God's world (Roms. 6:8-11; Acts 2:38).
They do this by the help of God's holy spirit. From their
relationship with Jesus they form his body.

> This incorporation [in Christ] is affected by the
> establishment of a personal relationship with Him
> -- a relation which affects our deepest dispo-
> sitions.[44]

We are members of one another (Rom. 12:46). The picture
the New Testament presents is of the church as a group
based on solidarity and love. All members are called to
transcend all tendencies of individualism. Believers become an organism like the amoeba--a one cell animal, but
never loses individual accountability to God and the community to which one belongs.

Roger Mehl summarizes this best when he writes:

> The work accomplished by God in Christ, the foun-
> dation of the church made possible by this work,

bear witness to the fact that God calls all men
[and women] and all nations to live with him, in
a new relation, in a covenant of Grace, in a
relation of confidence, of peace, of love, of
service and adoration. This new relationship
with God makes possible the results in a new
relationship of men [women] to each other, a
fraternity transcending all sociological differ-
entiations. The community is not reduced to a
mere aggregate of persons, since they are united
beyond everything that separates them, in a single body which creates such a unity as to make it
truly possible to speak of the church as of a
single man [woman] who grows towards perfection
so far as the bond between each believer and the
Lord is not broken. There is here a perfect
mutuality between persons and community even
though all members are not equivalent (1 Cor.
12:12ff), a diversity of ministries.[45]

Roger Mehl has captured the essential features of New

Testament theology. The major difference between the New

Testament and the African and Old Testament concept of a

person and community is basically two. They both were/are

historically, geographically and ethically limited. The

relationship between the Old Testament and the New Testa-

ment is not comparable to the relationship of Ghanaian

beliefs to the the New Testament theologically.

The New Testament (and for that matter christianity)

puts the relationship of person and community within the

context of the whole of creation. Other than these differ-

ences, their notions of solidarity or corporate personality

are parallel. This degree of similarity between the tradi-

tional African notion of person and community and that of

the Biblical view suggests that the African holistic ap-

proach in treatment to a person who is sick does offer

itself as a viable alternative.

Footnotes

[1] Clifford Geertz, *The Interpretation of Cultures* (New York: Basic Books, 1973), p. 127.

[2] Kofi Appiah-Kubi, *Man Cures, God Heals* (New York: Friendship Press, 1981), p. 7.

[3] Meyer Fortes, *The Web of Kinship Among the Tallensis* (London: Oxford University Press, 1949), p. 3.

[4] Benjamin Ray, *African Religions: Symbols, Rituals and Community* (New Jersey: Prentice-Hall Inc., 1976), p. 133.

[5] Mercy Aba Oduyoye, "The Value of African Religious Beliefs and Practices for Christian Theology" in Kofi-Appiah-Kubi and Virginia Tories (eds.), *African Theology En Route* (New York: Orbis Books, 1979), p. 111.

[6] A. Shorter, *African Culture and the Christian Church* (New York: Orbis Books, 1974), p. 60.

[7] John S. Pobee, *Towards an African Theology* (Nashville: Abingdon Press, 1979), p. 45.

[8] *Ibid.*

[9] *Ibid.*

[10] *Ibid.*, p. 44.

[11] *Ibid.*, p. 48.

[12] Meyer Fortes, *Web of Kinship*, p. 28.

[13] *Ibid.*

[14] Benjamin Ray, *African Religion*, p. 34.

[15] *Ibid.*, p. 137.

[16] *Ibid.*, p. 139.

[17] *Ibid.*, p. 140.

[18] *Ibid.*

28

[19]I. Sow, Anthropological Structures of Madness in Black Africa (New Jersey: Prentice-Hall Inc., 1976), p. 129.

[20]Ibid., p. 125.

[21]Ibid., p. 125.

[22]Robert Hogan, Personality Theory: Personalogy Tradition (New Jersey: Prentice-Hall Inc., 1979), p. 3.

[23]Robert Schreiter, Constructing Local Theologies (New York: Orbis Books, 1985), p. 58.

[24]Ibid.

[25]Robert Hogan, Personality Theory, p. 133.

[26]C.G. Jung, Two Essays on Analytical Psychology (New York: Meridan Press, 1956), pp. 166-67.

[27]Robert Hogan, Personality Theory, p. 133.

[28]Ibid.

[29]Paul Tournier, Four Best Books in One Volume (New York: Iverson-Norman, 1977), p. 102.

[30]Ibid., p. 103.

[31]Ibid., p. 104.

[32]Ibid.

[33]Ibid., p. 107.

[34]Ibid.

[35]Ibid., p. 108.

[36]Ibid.

[37]Ibid., p. 119.

[38]Roger Mehl, "The Biblical Understanding of Community and Person," Canadian Journal of Theology 5,6 (1959-1960): 222.

[39]Ibid., p. 223.

[40] Ibid.

[41] Ibid., p. 224.

[42] Ibid., p. 225.

[43] Ibid.

[44] Ibid., p. 226.

[45] Ibid., p. 227-228.

30

3. A TRADITIONAL AFRICAN CONCEPT AND CAUSES OF SICKNESS

The African's concept of sickness, its causes and
cures, is considered from herbal, social and religious-
ritualistic points of view. In this approach, the ritualistic aspects such as divination and sacrifice, and the
role of the community will be emphasized. This emphasis is
pivotol in attempting to evolve ways of caring for the sick
in Africa. Nelson S.T. Thayer seems to echo similar sentiments when he says;

> A book [any theology and/or discussion] that
> attempts to treat the subject of spirituality and
> pastoral care [in my case pastoral theology in
> Africa] must take seriously the cultural context
> with which pastoral care occurs. Pastoral care
> does not occur in a vacuum, but within a matrix
> of social processes. How the pastor perceives,
> experiences, and evaluates these processes will
> affect both the actions of pastoral care and the
> overall 'mood' in which pastoral care is carried
> out.[1]

The statement is true for Ghanaians as supported by
Kofi Appiah-Kubi that "it is very difficult for the average
Akan [Ghanaian] christian, therefore to sever all links
with his [her] culture."[2] This is a very important point
to note because some western-trained, sophisticated doctors
have unsuccessfully attempted to brand Ghanaian traditional
notions of sickness and their healers as superstitious,
ignorant, pagan, and even criminal. Some of these western-
trained doctors are losing the battle to the traditional-
ists. There are many reasons given and Kofi Appiah-Kubi
seems to offer the most significant:

that modern [western-trained] doctors and their
sophisticated modern medical centers have not
been able to meet the Akans' [Ghanaians'] health
needs, is that the most of these facilities have
been operating for years without reference to the
Akan concept of health and disease and their
general world view.

The problem is magnified by the huge numbers of quasi-
medical and faith healing shrines being established in
Africa. Even if their increasing numbers were not enough
to alert the western mission church that something is hap-
pening, the fact that some people leave the church hospitals, signals a deficiency in the approach of the christian
ministry of healing in Africa.

This book is not concerned with examining theories/-
hypotheses, concerning the causes of sickness, approaches
to the process of healing, and western medical diagnoses.
Instead, it will explore only the methodological approach.
The debate in medical circles about the clinical differences and/or similarities between sickness, illness and
disease, will not be pursued. Most of the examples will be
drawn from Ghana, with some relevant examples from other
African contexts.

In Africa, both good health and sickness can be likened to two sides of the same coin. Health, i.e., good
health, for Ghanaians, for example, is defined by Kofi
Appiah-Kubi as the

> well-being of mind, body and spirit; living in
> harmony with one's neighbour, the environment and

oneself and in all levels of reality--physical, social, spiritual, natural and supernatural.[4]

Therefore, health for Appiah-Kubi "is symptomatic of a correct relationship with one's environment."[5] To go back to the analogy of the Rubik Cube, health for Africans then means that all the cubes are where they are supposed to be. It also means that there is equilibrium in one's relationships.

Conversely then, sickness means that the Rubik Cube is shifted and the equilibrium is destablized. Sociologically, this could mean a relationship is strained by an act or acts in the family, clans and/or community of the offender. Religiously, it is interpreted as breaking or weakening the spiritual bond of protection, hence invoking the wrath of the ancestors, evil spirits and indeed all the harmful elements in the society.

The full effects of straining the one or various relationships of an individual and diminishing the spiritual protection could be translated physiologically into an ache or pain, i.e., some form of sickness in the body. Kwesi Dickson makes a helpful contrast between the western-trained doctors' notion of disease pathology and the traditional African notion of sickness or disease:

> Disease may be the result of invading bacteria and other micro-organisms, as the western trained doctor would explain it; the death of an old person from respiratory disorders may be the result of weakened body systems being unable to cope with the deleterious effects of, say, smog

in London or Los Angeles. To the African disease
and death are ultimately by spirits' powers.[6]

Another fundamental difference between the western-trained

doctor and the traditionalist view of the cause of sickness

is correctly pointed out by Kofi Appiah-Kubi that "the

sources of illness and health, lie beyond that which can be

felt and touched."[7] This, however, is not applicable to

all sicknesses.

Eugene Mendonsa provides an example from the Sisalas

of Northern Ghana:

> when a person suffers a snakebite, he immediately
> checks to see if it is poisonous. If it is not,
> he does not worry since the relationship between
> venom and death is well known. All events which
> are not specifically considered to be super-
> naturally caused, the Sisala first seek natural
> causal explanations before pursuing occult causes
> through divination. If a man's child is sick,
> the father tries local medicines before consult-
> ing the diviner. The diviner is normally only
> consulted when investigation of possible earthly
> causes and cures fail.[8]

Ghanaians also suffer from some seasonal sicknesses such as

colds during the "hamattan" and rainy seasons. The length

and the severity of the sickness cause Ghanaians to ques-

tion and look for causes outside the ordinary. For exam-

ple, the Tonises of Nigeria consider sickness as caused by

multiple factors; some are natural, others are super-

natural. For the Zulus of South Africa, sickness can be

umkhu lane - nje (light disease) or mkufa kwabantu (death,

a serious or fatal sickness. The Gas of Ghana believe the

cause of sickness is from the kla (personal soul) spirits and evil people.[9]

The African concept of sickness is both individual and cosmic. It may be caused by an individual not acting appropriately, i.e., violating the spiritual laws that bond him/her, thereby invoking a curse by the ancestors. The reasoning behind this concept for the Tallensis and probably most African communities suggests that

> a person cannot divest himself [herself] or be divested of the bonds created by his [her] birth and yet remain a member of the society nor can he [she] fully and unconditionally acquire these bonds except by birth.[10]

Furthermore, they strongly believe that

> one's bonds with one's lineage imply a ritual bond with one's patrilineal [matrilineal for the Akans and a section of the Ewes] ancestors and other mystical forces associated with the existence and well being of the lineage. They are the chief mystical powers governing the life of the individual.[11]

The sense of unity of all in the community and the sense of oneness with the community explain further why the Akans of Ghana share this belief that

> disease is believed to be sometimes caused by failure to perform the right religious act at the right time. Or the victim may not be the [direct] offender at all but rather may be suffering from the offense of a kinsman.[12]

This belief also explains why the role of one's family in an African sense is very vital in the process of healing. Together with the victim's community, the "treatment is person centred, in contrast to western style medicine, which is disease oriented."[13]

Another cause of sickness comes out of the African cosmology. Some detail on the cosmology is given in Chapter One. This view articulates the cause in a simple way: "Protecting spirits, evil spirits, supernatural monsters and magical spirits are real to Akans, forming a coherent system."[14] Sickness is seen as the "wickedness, tragedies and misfortunes of life."[15]

If, for example obayi in Akan or soi in Tallen, attacks an individual, that person could fall sick. Obayi or soi means an evil possessed person who has special powers to inflict harm on others. There are many reasons why a witch (obayi, soi) will attack someone. The commonest reason is that the witch is jealous of the victim's prosperity measured by the frequency of pregnancy of his wife or wives, the number of children, or in the case of a woman, the prosperity of her husband and children, and the quality of her general well-being. For Africans then,

> disease is an attack by a spirit upon one's spir-
> it and it can be overcome by medicine whose spir-
> it is stronger than the spirit of the disease.
> An illness that does not yield to such a medicine
> must be attributed to other forces, such as
> witchcraft. Religion is the means of counter-
> acting evil, or reinforcing life through proper
> precautions against destructive powers.[16]

There is another cause of sickness which prevails among the various communities in Northern Ghana. These communities believe that:

a breakdown in the relation between a person and
his shrine [in Tallen yin or seer which Meyer
Fortes and Horton misinterpret as destiny] 'which
is a manifestation of spiritual power' is thought
to lead to a breakdown in the relation between
one's body and soul.[17]

In all these cases, there is both the potentiality of

death or of restoration of good health. Where the sickness

deteriorates and death is inevitable, it does not take much

imagination to sense the tremendous anxiety, fear, sense of

guilt, failure and shame that is being experienced both

individually and corporately. This pressure is shared by

the family/clan members, not only because they are losing a

loved one, but also because of their own fears of becoming

victims if the causes are not detected and the right ritu-

als performed. As pointed out earlier, the Ghanaians'

concept of communitas ac societas unitae shows that they

believe that the consequences of one person's act in the

family can be suffered by all. The concept is perhaps

similar to the notion of the "iniquity of the father af-

fecting the children to the third and fourth generations"

(Deut. 5:9), also that of "the fathers have eaten sour

grapes and the children's teeth are set on edge" (Jer.

31:29, Ezek. 18:2) and the "sin of Achan" (Josh. 7:24).

This then is the basic concept of sickness and its causes

which has immediate relevance to the religious dimension of

Ghanaians.

AFRICAN APPROACH TO HEALING

The traditional approach to handling the sick in Africa, is to answer the immediate question of the sick, especially of those with a death threatening sickness, which is "why?". However, that is where the similarities to other cultures may end.

As suggested earlier, Africans traditionally would try initially to diagnose the sickness by reference to common causes and cures. When the sickness persists they have no choice but to be suspicious that there are deeper causes, hence deeper cures.

The African then proceeds to the diviner as his/her diagnostician. By definition, a diviner is a person who discloses the causes of misfortune and death. His job is not to foretell the future, but rather

> to scrutinize the past in order to identify the spiritual and human agents responsible for personal misfortunes. Since all human problems, such as infertility, illness..., are ascribed to moral conflicts within the human community, the diviner's task is to disclose acts of immorality which have provoked the vengeance of the ancestors and to reveal the destructive hand of witches and sorcerers.[18]

The notion of, or process of, divination is very important in this book because of its importance and role in the diagnosis and treatment of sickness in Ghana and indeed Africa as a whole. I. Sow's discussion of divination in Africa in general is also true of Ghana in particular. He makes an invaluable contribution when he writes,

in the realm of the traditional African diagnostician's operation and procedures, divination is
an important, though not an exclusive, facet of
his profession. So if we hope to understand the
meaning of concepts concerning sickness, it seems
essential that we try to grasp, at least in terms
of their basic principles, not only the concrete
operational modalities of divination but also the
conceptual associations of such practices within
the coherent universe of thought to which they
[Africans including Ghanaians] belong.[19]

This thesis will deal only with the "diagnostic inter-

pretation rather than that of physical divination involving

anatomy and physiology,"[20] based on I. Sow's approach. I.

Sow's approach is adopted because

what interests us for our present purpose is the
structure of the diagnostic divination in relation to the mentality of people seeking consultation.[21]

It is the aim of this author to explore ways of enhancing

the contribution of divination to pastoral theology. This

task is an important one from the point of view of the

definition of pastoral theology which is

...the study of all aspects of care of persons in
the church in a context of theological inqui-
ry....The aim of such a task is grubbing in the
root systems of human need and human hope with
the intent to strengthen, nurture and if possible
to   aid   development,   that   provides   the
particularity of pastoral theology and its
potential and actual contribution to theology.[22]

The discussion on divination will include the follow-

ing: a) How does and who becomes a diviner, b) Types of

divination, and c) The actual mechanics or dynamics of

divination.

a) Who and How One Becomes a Diviner

In most African communities, anyone in whose family or clan either maternally or paternally has ever been a diviner, can become one. In other words, it is partly inherited, but not through the genes. It is not everyone who becomes a diviner just by virtue of the fact that an individual's family or clan has had one or more diviners. One must always be chosen. The spirit of the ancestor who was a diviner must choose the individual.

There are normally signs shown by the potential diviner's behaviour indicating that something unusual has happened in his/her life. The signs may differ from community to community. They may range from severe psychotic behaviours to a mild change in mood with no change in life style at all. When this calling is recognized, tested and confirmed by the community, one goes into training.

The length, content and symbols of training differ according to the psychological setting of the candidate. Like the Yorubas in Nigeria, the candidates from some communities like the Tallensis, Sisalas, Dagombas of Northern Ghana "learn a prodigious amount of technical and oral knowledge,"[23] and learn to recite some incantations and perform some rituals. The most important part of the training is learning to submit to the spirit of the ancestor for direction, i.e., messages, meanings and also personal information. In divination, the fundamental assumption is that the spirit of the ancestor concerned is inspiring the diviner and is communicating with him/her in the process. A diviner is not necessarily always knowledgeable in herbs, hence, may not be a "medical" healer. One is not necessarily a prerequisite for the other. However, there are people who have knowledge of both. The duration of training varies according to one's previous experience and/or spiritual awareness before being called. It should be noted that one's excellence does not necessarily depend on the duration of training. One never fully graduates. One is considered a trainee in the "spiritual" matters in practice. One cardinal rule must always be observed by all: upright living in all its broadest meanings and implications. Generally one must be above twenty years of age before being initiated with an elaborate ritual involving the community of the dead and living.

b) **Types of Divination**

I. Sow's view is that the many forms and types of divination can be classified under two headings: Inspired divination and Deductive divination.

Adopting the definition of I. Sow, inspired divination includes:

> all techniques of so-called possession, aimed
> ultimately at plumbing the deeper psychic layers
> of professional adepts, adepts in states of
> trance induced and directed by a master.[24]

Deductive divination is the objective employing of a material vehicle and

> the diviner's task consists more narrowly, in terms of operations and interpretations, of examining the evidence (series of mantic configurations) and drawing conclusions therefrom, adhering rigorously to the internal logic and laws of the science of divination.
> It is a form of diagnostic or prophylactic counsel that anyone can seek at will, aimed at establishing a diagnosis or prognosis when a decision looms or illness strikes. This type of active divination interprets real events by analyzing the configurations of objects arranged by aleatory procedures or by reading ideographic or pictographic signs; it seeks to decipher the universe as if it were a question of a text in which one would find the order of the world inscribed, a tablet on which the gods would have traced out men's [women's] destinies.[25]

I. Sow, in describing the functions of the diviner, seems to be echoing Anton Boison's notion of studying the "human living document". Although one person under a given circumstance may exhibit either of these two ways, divination with reference to the latter notion will be used. If the former notion is used, it will be indicated specifically.

c) **Mechanics or Dynamics of Divination**

There is much literature on this subject. Two authors whose seminal works are the most accurate, up-to-date, and informative are: Benjamin C. Ray in his chapter entitled "Religious Authorities", subheaded "Diviners", from his book, <u>African Religions, Symbols, Rituals and Community</u>, and the western African psychiatrist I. Sow in his chapter, "The Position and Functions of the Therapist in the Traditional African Universe", in his book Anthropological Structures of Madness in Black Africa. When someone is sick, and the family/clan cannot determine a cause immediately, they assemble the elders, discuss the matter and decide which diviner to consult; then they turn the task over to the diviner. The diviner's

> task is to bring to light (and lay bare) the fundamental conflict that has caused the patient to be personally afflicted with one disorder or another under certain specific circumstances.[26]

I. Sow describes the tools of the diviner as

> all observable phenomena, relating to terrestrial or celestial elements, animal or human, physiological or psychological, animate or inanimate, [which] can serve as signs, the moon, sun, stars, rain, of the earth, sand, stones, shells (cowries), the use of vegetable matter, seeds, nuts, the use of animals, the use of such objects as knucklebones, dice, sticks, the use of the human body, with reference to facial features, etc.[27]

On the subject of the mechanics or processes used, I. Sow continues

> The seance develops in three successive stages to arrive at a synthesis establishing the final diagnosis, which at the same time, always provides an interpretation of the case as a whole:

> I. The mantic examination proper, consisting of detailed questioning of the different relational poles that form the very foundation of the patient's psychological makeup as person/personality, with interrogation in terms of pairs of opposites--stability (favourable) instability (unfavourable); in short, examination of the elements constituting the socio cosmic universe in which the supplant has his [her] roots, and precisely from which his [her] sickness (affliction) seems to uproot him.

II. Determination of a diagnosis through meaning, always followed by formulation of a prog-
nosis.

III. Prescription, that is indicating the methods of treatment and initiating the therapeutic
procedure.[28]

I. Sow makes an accurate analysis of divination. He

writes:

> In essence it will consist of bringing to light
> the unapparent, hidden elements that make up the
> conflict structure reflected in the clinical
> case, for mental as well as organic disorders and
> even in a general way, for unhappy experiences,
> including the failures encountered in everyday
> life.[29]

I. Sow's analysis seems to agree with the views of Paul

Tournier already mentioned in Chapter One. I. Sow further

makes an observation which partially undergirds the intent

of this thesis. He writes,

> In this sense, divination practiced...[by] ana-
> lyzing and interpreting an important social con-
> cern differs in no way, in terms of the substance
> and nature of the diviner's role, from the activ-
> ity of highly placed technocrats, manipulating
> mathematical models on the basis of data and
> weighing risks (intermediate or long-term) to
> make their forecasts and offer advice.[30]

It does not seem reasonable to equate a human problem to

mathematical models on the basis of data, nor to equate a

diviner with a technocrat.

Kofi Appiah-Kubi gives an example worth quoting which

emphasizes the role of the diviner in Ghana in spite of the

degree of western and/or christian influence in Ghana.

> Akosua and Amma were very good friends. Akosua
> started flirting with Amma's husband and the

result was an unexpected pregnancy. Akosua was
embarrassed but could not bring herself to confess to her friend. When Akosua was in labour,
she became very wild. The doctors helped her
deliver her baby, but after delivery, Akosua
became more violent and uncontrollable. The
doctors diagnosed a mental breakdown (psychosis)
and advised that she must be sent to a mental
hospital. After some weeks of observation and
treatment, Akosua was getting worse and worse,
and her family removed her to a traditional healer. Through divination, Akosua was brought to
confess her infidelity. Akosua's parents were
told to pacify her friend and ask for her forgiveness for the offence. Amma, at this stage,
had no alternative but to forgive her friend. A
sacrificial meal was prepared and Akosua and her
friend Amma, with a few of their relatives,
shared the meal. Akosua was purified of her
pollution, and peace was made between the two
friends and the families. Akosua is now back to
normal.[31]

As a kind of analysis Kofi Appiah-Kubi writes:

It is impossible to determine exactly how such an
approach to treatment works--as it does, in case
after case. But unquestionably the fact that it
attacks underlying problems, not merely symptoms,
is carried out in a meaningful context, and is
based on shared beliefs helps to explain its
success.[32]

Another example comes from a pastoral encounter.

There was an evangelical or conservative woman who had a

baby in Europe. The woman is the kind who believes in "the

Bible says". Consequently she sees Ghanaian culture as

pagan. However, one of the beliefs in Ghana is that a

newly delivered woman either covers her hair or shaves, to

ward off bad luck.

This couple thought they had outgrown the culture so

the woman went and had a hair-do to appear nice before her

western visitors. A day after, she began to feel head

aches. During my visit she complained that she had a head
ache so I asked whether she knew the cause. She quickly
replied, "If I were in the village I should have covered my
hair. Maybe, it is because I have had a hair do. Our
people know why they believe these things." This case
exemplifies the dualistic worlds of many christians in
Africa. While the cultural taboos, beliefs and practices
may be suspended or ignored or suppressed, they are hardly
forgotten or eliminated even by the Bible quoting christians, at least unconsciously.

The next approach to healing is the sacramental part
where the priest is directly involved in the healing pro-
cess-the sacrifice. There are many and varied reasons for
the rite of sacrifice. In some African dialects, they have
one word for both sacrifice and heal. For example, among
the Bahaya of central Africa, the word okutamba means both
to heal and to sacrifice. As correctly pointed out by
Sundkler, "This shows...originally the priest and the leech
or herbalist had a similar function and that religion and
medicine have sprung from a common root."[33] The discussion
of sacrifice here is limited to the sacrifice recommended
by the diviner as part of the diagnosis and process of
healing a sick person.

Sacrifices, according to Evans-Pritchard (a leading
anthropologist-ethnologist and a notable researcher and
writer on the Sisalas of Northern Ghana), can be classified

into two categories: confirmatory sacrifices and piacular sacrifices.

Confirmatory sacrifice "is chiefly concerned with the social relations--changes of social status and the inter-actions of social groups..."[34] This corresponds to those rituals involving sacrifices that are often referred to as rites of passage in some recent African writings on this subject.

The second category, piacular sacrifice, is

> concerned rather with the moral and physical welfare of the individual and is performed in situations of danger from the intervention of spirit in human affairs, often thought of as being [brought] about by some faults. In such sacrifices ideals of propitiation and expiation are prominent and their purpose described by words which have the sense of bargain, exchange and purpose.[35]

For the purpose of this book, the discussion will relate mainly to piacular sacrifice, which could be the Ghanaian equivalent of atonement rites in the Judeo-chris-tian sense. Among the Sisalas, the piacular sacrifice

> wese wiaa literally to 'repair thing' and con-notes expiation [and also] and act of begging for forgiveness or an apology. Piacular sacrifice is intended to amend a broken relationship.[36]

The motif for piacular sacrifice in Africa is exem-plified among the Tallensis of Northern Ghana by Meyer Fortes,

> The moral imperative of a ritual prohibition or injunction kiiher is connected with the de-pendence of the lineage of its ancestors' good-will for its survival and welfare. The emphasis

in their culture is on conduct, not on creed, on
performance rather than on doctrine.[37]

How Piacular Sacrifices are Carried Out

In most communities in Africa, the sacrifice will follow a formula briefly stated thus: usually, the diviner
prescribes the sacrifice of an animal with or without unique features. The family or clan obtains the animal with
locally brewed beer. The degree of elaborateness of prescription can indicate the seriousness of the offence, the
sickness and the chances of survival. The family/clan
assembles at the house of the head of the family/clan with
various representatives of the family branches or yizug.
The clan head normally is also the oldest member of the
clan and the priest as well.

i) He (usually a man in most of the communities in
Ghana) presides, recites a long litany of the names of the
ancestors with praises especially for the heroes, and men-
tions as many names of the living as possible.

ii) He states the reason why they have assembled.

iii) He makes a confession for all the clan followed
by petitions. The victim, the one sick, is particularly
mentioned by name.

iv) The animal is killed, the blood is smeared on the
shrine. The meat is cut and shared. Some is cooked and
eaten in a ritualistic way. Every representative must eat

the cooked meat. It may or may not involve ritual washing. When the meat is being eaten or before consuming it, the senior member of the clan and the priest invoke healing, forgiveness and blessing on all members of the clan. The incantations at the sacrifice are believed to carry with them the power to effect what they are intended to do, i.e., bring healing, forgiveness, blessing.

Comments

This chapter has been concerned with the concept of sickness, its causes, the process of divination as a diagnosis of healing, and sacrifice as a process of healing. To build on the concept discussed above, this conceptual framework will be developed here, but not through western medical or psychological perspectives. The rule of internal logic, which tries to see things from their psychocultural mileau, no matter how absurd they might appear to a foreign viewpoint or a multiperspectival view influenced by western culture, christian theology, and scientific critical thinking is observed here. Comparisons will be made when and if necessary.

It has been argued that the African notion of sickness is moralistic. Authors like Meyer Fortes, Margaret Field, Benjamin Ray, to name just a few, fall into this category. Although there is definitely a strong religious aspect in the Ghanaian concept, it is not moralistic. Religious

beliefs by their nature imply some form and degree of mo-
rality, but the Ghanaian notion of sickness cannot be said
to be totally moralistic. What has mistakenly coloured
this interpretation is the many examples of dos and don'ts
in African societies. In every tale, story, drama, song
and ritual, there is an implication of a do and/or a don't.
However, even the western world is not free from dos and
don't as preventive medicine. On the contrary, George M.
Foster suggests that the western world, in spite of preventive innoculations, still has dos and don'ts. George M.
Foster writes:

> Preventive medicine, insofar as it refers to
> individual oriented behaviour, can be thought of
> as a series of 'dos' and 'don'ts' or 'shoulds'
> and 'shouldn'ts'. In contemporary America we
> 'should' get our physical examination, our eyes
> ...checked regularly, and make sure our immuniza-
> tions are up to date...We should not smoke cigar-
> ettes, breathe polluted air,...or engage in a
> series of other activities known or believed to
> be inimical to health. In all other societies
> similar 'shoulds' and 'shouldn'ts' can be identi-
> fied.[38]

With this parallel, the African notion of sickness cannot
be said to be simply moralistic. Two principles of ana-
lyzing the African notion of sickness given by George M.
Foster are helpful. He gives "two principal etiologies" of
sickness: namely, "personalistic" and "naturalistic".
According to Foster,

> A personalistic medical system is one in which
> disease is explained as due to the active pur-
> poseful intervention of an agent, who may be
> human (a witch or sorcerer), nonhuman (a ghost,

an ancestor, an evil spirit), or supernatural (a
deity or other very powerful being). The sick
person literally is a victim, the object of ag-
gression or punishment directed specifically
against him. Abron [a tribe in the Ivory Coast
sharing borders with Ghana, like all Ghanaians]
theory contains a host of agents which may be
responsible for a specific condition...these
agents cut across the natural and supernatural
world.
        In contrast to personalistic systems, natu-
ralistic systems explain illness in impersonal,
systemic terms. Disease is thought to stem, not
from the machinations of an angry being, but
rather from such natural forces or conditions as
cold...by an upset in the balance of basic body
elements.[39]

Therefore in Africa, sickness is seen as predominently per-

sonalistic. However, the warning of George M. Foster is

worth taking seriously. He warns that

    the two etiologies are rarely if ever mutually
    exclusive as far as their presence or absence in
    a particular society is concerned.[40]

He points out one main difference which can be seen as a

cutting edge between the two:

    In personalistic systems illness is but a special
    case in the explanation of all misfortune. Some
    societies [quoting Horton] have adopted a 'per-
    sonal idiom' as the basis of their attempt to
    understand the world, to account for almost ev-
    erything that happens in the world, only acciden-
    tally including illness. In naturalistic sys-
    tems, disease etiologies are disease specific,
    other areas of misfortune, such as personal quar-
    rels not surprisingly explained in personalistic
    terms.[41]

    Foster further helps in the understanding of the Afri-

can approach from the personalistic category. He writes:

    It should be noted too, that most of these acts
    [divination and sacrifice] conform to a general
    pattern in which aid of supernaturals is sought

for any kind of misfortune, such as illness or
accident. All causality is general and compre-
hensive and not specific to illness but paradoxically, when ritual supplications and sacrifices
are made, usually they are narrowly limited in
scope, specific to a particular illness or to
prevent feared illness.[42]

To facilitate further comparisons and a better summary of

the discussion so far, a summary chart by George M. Foster

should prove useful:

Figure 1

SUMMARY OF THE TWO SYSTEMS OF DISEASE ETIOLOGY
AND THEIR CORRELATES[43]

System	Personalistic [Ghanaian]	Naturalistic western without native Indians
Causation	Active Agent	Equilibrium loss
Illness	Specific cause of misfortune	Unrelated to other misfortunes
Religion, magic	Intimately tied to illness	Largely unrelated to illness
Causality	Multiple levels	Single level
Prevention	Positive action	Avoidance
Responsibility	Beyond patient control	Resides with patient

The constructs represented above briefly can be summarized
by Evans-Pritchard's graph.[44]

Figure 2

Supernatural	Non-Supernatural
Ultimate Causes	Immediate Causes

Siejas' analysis of the chart in Figure 2 is very similar

to Foster's. According to Siejas

> supernatural causes are those which place the
> origin of the disease with supra-sensible forces,
> malevolent agents or acts which are not directly
> observable.[45]

In this category, witches, evil spirits, demons, are offer-

ed as explanations for causes.

> Non-supernatural disease etiologies are those
> based wholly on observed cause-and-effect rela-
> tionships regardless of the accuracy of the ob-
> servations made. The diagnosis that an indiv-
> idual's malaise is due to profuse bleeding from a
> wound is based on a non-supernatural theory of
> causation as is the observation that this same
> individual dies as a consequence of swelling
> located at the point of lesion which moved up to
> his heart thereby killing him.[46]

<u>N.B.</u> By reproducing the above, the implication is not

necessarily agreement with every item contained in the

comparisons of these charts.

With regard to this sacrifice and the sacrificial

meal, the act of sacrifice is a sacrament in most African

communities. A definition of sacrament given by Joseph

Martos is a useful working one:

> Sacraments in all religions [including tradi-
> tional religion in Ghana] function as 'doors to
> the sacred' that is as invitations to religious
> experiences. Such experiences <u>hierophanies</u>, from
> the Greek words <u>hieros</u> meaning sacred or holy,
> and <u>phano</u>, meaning to manifest or reveal. A
> <u>hierophany</u> then, is a manifestation of the sa-
> cred, an experienced revelation of the holy.
> Having such an experience is like entering into
> another dimension of space and time and dis-
> covering a whole new world meaning.[47]

Benjamin Ray sees the sacrificial animal as a bridge; "it

[the animal] combines certain symbolic features which link

the human with the divine."[48] Furthermore,

> the offering [of the animal] thus symbolizes the
> return of the lineage to the right values of
> order and right relationship and behaviour, that
> is to the immortal 'word' of the ancestors which
> are its guiding norms. It implies that the so-
> cial conflict within the community is now re-
> solved.[49]

The notion of the scapegoat and the substitutional theory

of atonement "...He took our infirmities and bore our dis-

eases" (Matt. 8:17) is echoed here.

The incantations during the sacrifice are a very im-

portant aspect of the sacrifice. Benjamin Ray suggests

that:

> The verbal component of the sacrifice, the 'word'
> also serves to control this transaction by in-
> fluencing the gods, through prayer and song to
> act on man's behalf.[50]

The effect of the word in the sacrifice with respect to

healing, is similar to the centurion's plea to Jesus for

the healing of his slave. "...But say the word, and let my

servant be healed" (Lk. 7:7, Matt. 8:8) and Christ's cast-

ing out the demons "with a 'word' and healed all who were

sick" (Matt. 8:16, RSV).

The sharing of the meal is also worth noting. Ben-

jamin Ray seems to echo, partially, its intent, when he

says,

> The sharing of the victim's flesh confirms the
> spiritual bond between the worshippers and the
> god and spirits to whom a portion is given.[51]

However, Meyer Fortes' views of its meaning and function among the Tallensis of Ghana is best. Fortes writes:

> To sacrifice 'kab, kaabera' is the most binding form of ritual collaboration. To sacrifice together means not only to acknowledge common spiritual tutelage but also to eat together of all the sacrifice, in short is to unite in a sacrament. Thus, it is both an expression and a pledge of mutual amity and dependence.[52]

These few pages have provided not only a brief description of the African approach to healing but also have attempted to establish a conceptual framework through the eyes of ethnology, with some comparisons and insights from the religious dimension which is essential to this christian ministry of healing in Africa.

To conclude this section, a view by David Bakan in his chapter, "The Paradox of the Function of Pain" in Disease, Pain and Sacrifice, first published in 1968, but by no means out-of-date thereby, will be adopted:

> Pain in its final analysis is a warning signal against potential or actual damage, produces the outcry which evokes help by others. The sounds caused by pain which are made by infants and even adults are part of a universal language of man, transcending all cultural differences and have the singular meaning of 'help'.[53]

To Africans, the psycho-social and spiritual approach is deemed an appropriate response to their cry for "help!". Consequently, for the church in Africa, the cultural milieu is the starting point for providing relevant christian theology in general, and christian pastoral care in particular, especially if those crying are christians. While the interpretation of the African concept and causes and/or treatment of sickness solely in terms of moralistic terms is to be objected to, there is definitely a dynamic relationship in traditional African thought between moral evil and physical evil. One causes the other; the presence of one necessitates the possible presence of the other. It is worth mentioning that studies in depth psychology and psychosomatic medicine support this view. Richard Yadeau seems to support this notion when he writes that "the patient is not a disease entity or medical problem to be treated with surgery, radiation or chemotherapy."[54] Hence he concludes that

> healing is a process of profound dimensions,
> involving virtually all aspects of a person's
> life--physical, spiritual, psychological, social
> dimensions, environmental and even political.[55]

Therefore, the holistic approach to healing and/or the ministry for the sick in Africa has much to contribute to a highly compartmentalized western culture and to pastoral care in particular.

The modern christian church in Africa must move beyond the early missionary approach to labelling everything they did not understand about African culture as suspicious and demonic. It is becoming clear, in recent times at least, that no one community or group of communities has a monopoly on the truth, nor has devised completely sufficient ways of dealing with the intricacies, or better still, mysteries of life.

Daniel J. Simundson raises some very fundamental questions which are often heard at the bedside, in the healing
shrines and even in the homes of African christians when
they are sick. Some of these questions are:

> If Jesus comes to heal the sick, why does He not
> heal me? Is my illness a sign that I have done
> something wrong for which God [and latent in
> their mind a witch, or their ancestors] are pun-
> ishing me? Does not God care about me anymore?
> If God heals those who have faith, does that mean
> that my faith is inadequate? My Bible quoting
> friends tell me to go directly to God for heal-
> ing? How can I pray?[56]

And, in some cases, some people ask the ultimate question,
whether or not they should remain christian(s) at all.
These questions are asked by many humans in different ways,
at different stages of their lives and in different cultures. Underlying all these questions is the fact that
sickness is a crisis of meaning because

> Like a stab in the dark, it comes upon us often
> without warning, as a sudden pain or disability
> that throws us off balance. Disturbing as it is
> to the comfort and freedom of living, it may also
> defeat one's life plans and cripple one's life
> powers. One is never ready for illness. It is
> always inconvenient, often unacceptable and in-
> tolerable either to bear in the anguish ongoing
> course of life. It is a blow that shatters the
> security of life.[57]

It is a time of great anxiety but "the basic anxiety of all
is the threat of nonbeing as one confronts ultimate loss of
all temporary gains."[58]

These fears and anxieties during times of sickness
have influenced the emphasis on the "meaning" component of

sickness. Therefore, for most Africans in general but particularly for christians, the "meaning" part should be taken seriously in any attempt to minister to our sick. This is because the western-trained doctor, with his/her sole biophysical approach and pharmaco-medical equipment, offers an incomplete approach in the treatment of some of the sick in Africa.

Footnotes

[1]Nelson S.T. Thayer, Spirituality and Pastoral Care (Philadelphia: Fortress Press, 1985), p. 15.

[2]Kofi Appiah-Kubi, Man Cures, God Heals (New York: Friendship Press, 1981), p. 5.

[3]Ibid., p. 3.

[4]Ibid., p. 8.

[5]Ibid., p. 14.

[6]Kwesi Dickson, Theology in Africa (New York: Orbis Books, 1984), p. 50.

[7]Kofi Appiah-Kubi, Man Cures, God Heals, p. 14.

[8]Eugene L. Mendonsa, "The Soul and Sacrifices Among the Sisala", Journal of Religion in Africa, 8 ((date unknown) Fase 1.

[9]B.G.M. Sundkler, Bantu Prophets in South Africa, (London: Oxford University Press, 1961), p. 101ff.

[10]Meyer Fortes, The Web of Kinship Among the Tallensis (London: Oxford University Press, 1949), pp. 21-22.

[11]Ibid., p. 48.

[12]Kofi Appiah-Kubi, Man Cures, God Heals, p. 14.

[13]Ibid.

[14]Ibid., p. 12.

[15]Ibid.

[16]Ibid.

[17]Eugene L. Mendonsa, "The Soul and Sacrifices Among the Sisalas", Journal of Religion in Africa, p. 55.

[18]Benjamin Ray, African Religion: Symbols, Rituals and Community (Englewood Cliffs, New Jersey: Prentice-Hall Inc., 1976), p. 104.

[19]I. Sow, Anthropological Structures of Madness in Black Africa (New York: International Universities Press Inc., 1980), pp. 57-58.

[20]Ibid., p. 56.

[21]Ibid.

[22]James Lapsley, Practical Theology and Pastoral Care: An Essay in Pastoral Theology in Don Browning (ed.), Practical Theology (San Francisco: Harper and Row, 1983), p. 167-171.

[23]Benjamin Ray, African Religion: Symbols, Rituals and Community, p. 10.

[24]I. Sow, Anthropological Structures of Madness in Black Africa, pp. 57-58.

[25]Ibid., p. 63.

[26]Ibid., p. 78-79.

[27]Ibid.

[28]Ibid., p. 65.

[29]Ibid.

[30]Ibid.

[31]Kofi Appiah-Kubi, Man Cures, God Heals, p. 76.

[32]Ibid.

[33]B.A.M. Sundkler, Bantu Prophets in South Africa, p. 221.

[34]E.E. Evans-Pritchard, "The Meaning of Sacrifice Among the Nuers", Journal of the Royal Anthropological Society 84 (1954): 21.

[35]Ibid.

[36]Eugene L. Mendonsa, "The Soul and Sacrifices Among the Sisalas", Journal of Religion in Africa 8: 63.

[37]Meyer Fortes, The Dynamics of Clanship Among the Tallensis, pp. 22, 130.

[38]George M. Foster, "Disease Etiologies in Non-Western Medical Systems", American Anthropologist 78 (1976): 779.

[39] Ibid., p. 775.

[40] Ibid., p. 776.

[41] Ibid., pp. 776-77.

[42] Ibid., pp. 777-78.

[43] Ibid.

[44] H. Sieja, "An Approach to the Study of Medical Aspects of Culture", Current Anthropology (1973): 544-45.

[45] Ibid.

[46] Ibid.

[47] Joseph Martos, Doors to the Sacred (New York: Image Books, 1982), pp. 14, 16.

[48] Benjamin Ray, African Religion: Symbols, Rituals and Community, p. 79.

[49] Ibid., p. 84.

[50] Ibid., p. 79.

[51] Ibid.

[52] Meyer Fortes, Dynamics of Clanship (London: Oxford University Press, 1945), p. 98.

[53] David Bakan, Disease, Pain and Sacrifice (Chicago: University of Chicago, 1968), p. 69.

[54] Richard E. Yadeau, "Healing", Word and World 2(5) (Fall, 1982): 319.

[55] Ibid.

[56] Daniel J. Simundson, "Health and Healing in the Bible", Word and World 2(4) (Fall, 1982): 330.

[57] Paul Johson, Psychology of Pastoral Care: The Pastoral Ministry in Theory and Practice (New York: Abingdon Press, 1953), p. 194.

[58] Paul Tillich, Courage To Be (New Haven: Yale University Press, 1952), p. 54.

4. EXPLORATION OF SOME OF THE PRINCIPLES AND PRACTICES OF PASTORAL CARE TO THE SICK IN THE WEST

First, an historical exploration of the salient principles and practices of pastoral care for the sick will be made. The purpose here is to help the church in Africa to gain both knowledge and warnings against some of the mistakes of the west. In order that this task does not go beyond the scope of this book, the parameters will be set by defining and discussing the following topics: principles and practices, pastoral care, the sick, and the west.

a) Principles and Practices

By principles and practices is meant how the christian church viewed illness or sickness and how ministers understood their ministry in relation to those who were sick. A description of the principles themselves in detail will not be given as that would be outside the main thrust of this chapter, but a brief summary of the predominant ideas as they relate to the healing ministry will be given.

b) Pastoral Care

By pastoral care is meant the shepherding aspect of the ministry as opposed to the teaching and preaching aspect. One may lead to the other and in practice it is not always easy to divide neatly the function of the minister's responsibility. Pastoral care as defined by Wayne Oates will be a working definition: "The christian pastor's combined fortification and confrontation of persons as persons in times of both emergency crisis and developmental crisis."[1] In this definition, interest is placed in the times of emergency crisis as opportunities for fortification defined as "to comfort, to strengthen, encourage, to support, sustain, put heart into".[2]

c) **The Sick**

By the word sick, is implied an "emergency crisis" in the body, sick in terms of the physiological connotation which may be apparent or real, temporary pain. Mental illness will be excluded as much as possible in this discussion of the sick.

d) **The West**

The term west within the christian context, especially in this historical context, means more than its present usage. However, the paper will not review the division of the church into east and west. Even though, in the historical survey, the period of the church that pre-dates the division mentioned will be touched upon, emphasis will be placed primarily on the period after the division. The word west is used to include Europe and North America. In the Reformation period, concentration will be placed on the Protestant tradition, and even more specifically, the Presbyterian tradition. The others will be mentioned in passing, when and if necessary for this purpose.

To attempt any historical survey of pastoral care is almost an impossible task because of the enigmatic nature of pastoral care. This is well articulated by Clebsch and Jaekle:

> Pastoral care has been exercised on innumerable occasions and in every conceivable human circumstance. Pastors rude and barely plucked from paganism, pastors sophisticated in the theory and practice of their profession, and pastors at every stage of adeptness between these extremes, have sought and wrought to help troubled people overcome their troubles.[3]

This attempt is a bird's-eye-view to summarize the uniqueness of each epoch of pastoral care within its own unique socio-political, cultural, human ecclesiastical and theological context.

According to McNeil, Clebsche and Jaekle, the first period of christianity emphasized the pastoral function of sustaining to the christians. The church was beginning to have its own identity and ethics. Like any society, the early church needed unity; unity among its members in word and deed. If there was any life style that would characterize them, it was upright living. Hence the preoccupation was with disciplinary measures and methods of repentance and acceptance. These new christians had experienced "new life in Christ". However, the physical limitations of their bodies and the attractiveness of "mundane" things paradoxically created much conflict in their life and faith.

The leaders became concerned with discipline among their followers. The emphasis on a strict discipline may have also been precipitated by their need to recommend themselves (the christian community) as worthy of being taken seriously by the society at large. Clebsch and Jaekle call the theme of this period of pastoral care 'sustaining'. The sustaining aspect of pastoral care became dominant primarily due to the early christians sense of the imminent return of Christ (Matt. 24:42). This does not mean that that there was no ministry of healing for the sick at all.[5]

Most of the literature available seems to echo the insights of Clebsch and Jaekle that

> healings occurred by way of imitating the curative thaumaturgy exercised by the Lord Himself, but these healings were valued rather as they displayed the power of Christ and his followers than as they ameliorated the plight of the sick and maimed.[6]

It also seems from these authors that there was direct connection between sin and sickness. The "cure of souls" was mainly directed to the spiritual aspect of a person. There was little need to relate one's spiritual life with the whole body. The christians of this period lived by the gospel of Jesus preached to them by a form of spiritual reductionism. The body was only a corrupt entity which if the _parousia_ delayed longer would only prove to be a liability. This approach to the christian life was later

articulated in books like The Imitation of Christ by Thomas
A. Kempis, and The Pilgrim's Progress by John Bunyan in the
sixteenth century.

The following era of the christian church after this
period was the era of oppression and persecution. By this
time the church leaders had strong believers, if not fana-
tic believers in another sense. The result of rigorous
discipline was an uncompromising militant church. They not
only became a distinct people in their communities, but
also a force to be reckoned with by the authorities. The
times of the pax Romana were over and difficult times for
the church lay ahead.

In the era of the persecution, many lost their lives
and many were thrown into prisons and tortured. For some
christians their mere existence was threatened if they
still held to their christian faith. Consequently, the
christian pastoral ministry changed emphasis. McNeil calls
this new emphasis "exhortation to faithfulness" and "comfort". Clebsch and Jaekle refer to this emphasis as "re-
conciling". Both views emphasize the need to encourage
believers to stand firm in their belief unto death. Death
for the sake of one's faith in Christ was the highest price
one could pay to gain entrance into God's kingdom. The
division between body and spirit and the belief that the
body is only a temporary container of the spiritual dimension was also prevalent in this period.

In this period there were also two concepts of sickness leading to two theologies:

1) That there were natural courses of life and that both the good people and the bad people share them. This is evidenced in St. Cyprian's exhortation to the christians when a plague or an epidemic broke out. He exhorted those who wavered in their faith during the epidemic that, "In all matters we share the perils of life with them, as in famine or common diseases. The difference is the faith that steadies us."[7]

2) That it was a sign of the end times which tested the faithful. The faithful should not be frightened. They (diseases) are tests. The gold is from the wood, the stone from the sand, and the grain separated from the cheff by these signs of the end times. Since life was transient, the stewardship of time, place, as resources for other things whilst waiting for the parousia made sickness a non-issue in this period of the church. For Cyprian

> the terrible symptoms of the disease may be matched by the strength of a mind unshaken. Christians who die escape miseries, corruptions and the fear of persecution. Men are tested by calamity and it is discovered whether they [love] the sick, whether men love their kindred...[8]

3) In the latter part of this quotation, there emerges a third concept of sickness as an opportunity to prove one's christian love and responsibility towards one another.

The period of persecution was followed by a period
which Clebsch and Jaekle called the "christian culture".
This period, according to Clebsch and Jaekle, began in the
reign of Constantine in the fourth century. Clebsch and
Jaekle believe that this era was one of

> fusing christianity and classical civilization
> into Greek-speaking Christendom.   The pastoral
> function now emphasized guiding.   The cure of
> souls sought to deal with the vast range of per-
> sonal problems, presented by a church membership.
> The ministry of healing concentrated upon anoint-
> ing with holy oil, and the ministry of recon-
> ciling became largely a matter of administering
> and enforcing standard church policies.[9]

It is worth noting that although the ministry of healing was never totally absent in the church, it was predominant only in times of relative peace.   Pastors in this
period were more like diviners in the way they ministered
to the sick and troubled.[10]

McNeil agrees with Clebsch and Jaekle that the period
following Constantine can be referred to as the "Medieval
christendom".   During this period the ministry of healing
developed and gained prominence in theology and practice.
Contemporary christians believed in the power of divine
grace to heal the soul and the body from what McNeil calls
"inherent and incidental deformities of human existence."[11]
For the church, the

> ministers imparted this healing by means of ob-
> jective, sacramental embodiment of that grace.
> The medieval parish became the compact, inclu-
> sive, geographical-social entity in which lived
> men and women of every sort and condition, to who

the parish priest dispensed medicines as they
needed for bodily or spiritual health. The Mass
provided grace more generally for the times of
temptation, disease, demon possession[12] moral
frailty, important decision...joy or woe.

Bishop Burchard was one who was described as diagnosing

spiritual illnesses and prescribing their treatment.[13]

The belief that spiritual healing will result in phys-

ical healing began to grow stronger. Hence the Fourth

Lateran Council ordered that

> when physicians of the body are called to the
> bedside of the sick, before all else, they admon-
> ish them to call for the physician of souls, so
> that after spiritual health has been restored to
> them, the application of bodily medicine may be
> of greater benefit.[14]

Their emphasis was not on the physical healing of the oils

and wines used; rather they believed in the potency of the

wine and oil as sacramental powers of healing. The ques-

tion whether the wine and oil acquired power to heal or

they depended on the faith of the christians is not ad-

dressed sufficiently. The research of Joseph Martos into

the healing ministry lends itself to this view, as quoted

by him:

> Around the middle of the century, Serapion the
> bishop of Thmuis in Egypt, composed a prayer for
> the blessing of oil, bread, and water, that they
> might, through the power of God, become a means
> of removing every sickness and disease, or ward-
> ing off every demon, of routing every unclean
> spirit, of keeping away every evil spirit, of
> banishing every fever, chill and fatigue...a
> medicine of life and salvation bringing health
> and soundness of soul and body and spirit, lead-
> ing to perfect well being.[15]

Another document called the "Apostolic Constitutions",

alleged to have been compiled in Syria, has the same notion of the potency for power in the blessed oil and water, given by God to bring the sick to health and to drive out demons.

At this stage in the church, there was a clear link between sin and sickness. Perhaps it was this belief or the discovery of this connection that gave rise to the highly developed penitential sacraments for the sick in the Roman Church, which regrettably are almost lost in some Reformed churches. It was this approach to holistic healing that gave impetus to orders like the Franciscans and Dominicans. These orders became interested in the holistic ministry to the sick or weak. The founder of the Franciscan order, Francis of Assisi, is a glowing example of one who devoted himself to this ministry of healing.

It is agreed by most church historians that the Middle Ages was a golden age for the christian church. It was this theological dominance over other disciplines that gave rise to the axiom that "theology is the queen of the sciences". It was not long, however, before the privileged position of theology, particularly pastoral theology to the sick, began to be challenged. It was during the Renaissance, that period of rebirth in learning, that the discoveries in science made theology seem eventually irrelevant.

There is little known of the nature and the emphasis of pastoral care in between. The anointing of the sick, prayers and pastoral visitations to the faithful continued, though in low profile alongside the care of physicians, surgeons and other paramedical disciplines.

At the time of the Reformation, the church had moved from under-utilization of the sacrament of anointing to its abuse. It took on commercial and political interests rather than sacramental. This abuse partially explains why the anointing of the sick was discontinued in some of the Reformed traditions.

In Lutheranism, the belief that the spiritual healing could result in physical healing prevailed. Luther's words in the official confessions of the Lutheran tradition as quoted by Martin E. Marty supports this. "We must regard the sacrament as a pure, wholesome, soothing medicine which aids and quickens us in both soul and body. For where the soul is healed, the body has benefited also."[16]

At the time of Zwingli, pastoral care had come to mean nurturing and teaching. Those who broke away from the Roman Catholic tradition argued that the church must be as a spotless spouse of Jesus renewed and sustained by God's spirit. Healing had come to mean teaching and nurturing persons away from the corrupt faith of the Roman Catholic practices. Hence, Zwingli warned the pastor to "be alert to prevent the sheep that is healed from falling again into sickness."[17] Zwingli was speaking of Protestant converts from Roman Catholic heresy as he saw it rather than bodily ailments. The predominant emphasis of pastoral care in this period was similar to the early times of the church fathers. Sickness was synonymous to sin. The Medieval anointing with wine and oil was replaced by emphasis on repentance, confession and forgiveness through faith in Christ. The role of scripture also became prominent in pastoral care.

In John Calvin's writings on visitation of the sick, pastoral care is given little or no emphasis. Apparently, reacting to the abuse of some of the sacraments in general including the anointing of the sick, Calvin says, "God is our physician".[18] His use of physician may refer to the forgiveness of sins rather than healing bodily ills. This is not to suggest that Calvin did not see the need for human beings to be co-workers or agents of God. Indeed, Calvin insisted that pastoral care is the duty of the whole community of the faithful. Thus pastoral care according to Calvin must be undertaken by both laity and clergy in the church. A cursory look at the theological writings of that time do not suggest any particular style of pastoral care to the sick.

John Calvin's tools of pastoral care were based on prayer and the Bible. The operative driving force of these tools was the individual faith of the believer, and his/her

total dependence on the Holy Spirit to help believers. In
his writings, John Calvin quotes Bible verses such as Mark
11:24—believe that what God promises He will do; James
1:5-6—promise to ask what we need; Matt. 8:13, 9:29—need
to ask in faith; 1 Tim. 2:5, Heb. 8:6 and 1 John 2:1—pray-
ing in the name of Jesus as our mediator to the Father.

In the anointing of the sick, Calvin did not object to
the use of oils. What he objected to was the exclusive
belief in the wine and oils as magically efficacious. He
believed that they could be effective if these elements
were accepted in faith. However, Calvin preferred that the
word of God, which is light and life, be used. He objected
to the use of the sacrament over and above the word of God.
For Calvin, one was no more effective than the other. He
was of the view that the sacraments have no effect in themselves unless they and the recipients are acted upon by the
Holy Spirit who helps the person to respond and be recep-
tive to the Grace of God.

The tradition of non-sacramental (not anointing with
oil) pastoral care to the sick has followed the Presbyterian tradition to date. Up to the time of John Knox, the
main focus of pastoral care was 'discipline'; the reform-
er's chief purpose was the nurturing of believers and the
fellowship of the faithful. During this period, there are
no detailed specific writings on how to care pastorally for
the sick. Probably the abuse of the sacrament of anointing

the sick haunted the Reformers so much that they were afraid to formulate anything in place of it. Another reason was the emphasis on personal faith in Jesus Christ rather than the reception of Grace through the medium of oil or priest. There was also the greater emphasis on the Bible as the sole rule of faith. The notion of vocation also gave physicians a place in the theology of Presbyterianism. They were considered to have been given the gifts of healing, hence their vocation.

However, there was also implicitly the sharp division between spirit and body. The medical doctors were baptised into christian care for the sick in the name of "the priesthood of all believers". The christian ministry became a ministry for every believer. They (christian ministers) ordained mainly for the word and sacrament. The designation minister verbi divini (servant of the word of God) replaced the sacramental notion of priesthood in the papal church. One could get the impression that the sick were pastorally neglected, left solely to the care of medical doctors and without prayers and visitations. All it means, however, is that there was no particularized instruction for the care of the sick. The pastoral ministry to the sick was done for the most part covertly, though at other times overtly. Apart from the Anglo-Catholic tradition which kept some sacramental theology for the sick and dying. Reformers like the Baptists, Congregationalists,

Methodists, and others followed more or less the pattern of ministry outlined above in the Presbyterian tradition. The main form of ministry to the sick in the Reformed tradition, especially the Presbyterian tradition, was by prayers and scriptural readings, the presence of the minister and the periodical communion (bread and wine) shared by all members of the congregation as the body of Christ.

The next period in the history of the West was the Enlightenment. In the period of the Enlightenment (16th to 18th centuries) theology ceased to be the "queen of the sciences"--though not absent in practice and in the university curricula. This trend continued to the beginning of the twentieth century. The churches lost much of their moral influence on the populace. The mood of this period was best summarized in our own era in the alleged words of Dr. Martin Luther King, Jr., namely that "Scientists have become the priests and the prophets, and the laboratories are the cathedrals."[19] The personality sciences also grew as psychology more or less replaced theology for many people. The individual became the focus of attention rather than the community. In this situation arose the "God is dead" literature. Many factors such as the political revolutions, internal splits and quarrelling in the churches, the writings of Karl Marx, the great scientific achievements, the World Wars, etc., contributed to this decline in the prominence of theology.

Theology divided into schools and disciplines independent of each other. Pastoral theology was caught in the
confusion. Some theologians maintained that pastoral theology which referred to all that a minister did, while
others argued that it referred to the content of the time
spent with someone in trouble. These divisions may have
contributed to pastoral theology in particular and christian theology in general and to the exodus of people from
the churches. Meanwhile, psychological explanations for
people's problems gained currency.

Psychology, or the scientific approach to the sick,
had influenced pastoral care by the turn of the century--an
important factor in this book which is both an attempt to
evolve an approach to pastoral care for the sick in Africa,
and a critique of the predominant scientific approach to
the sick in the western world.

A brief survey of pastoral theology is appropriate
here, with emphasis on the sick in Western Europe at the
turn of the century. A name usually associated with pastoral theology in Europe is Friederich Schleiermacher (1768-
1834). He is referred to by some scholars as the father of
pastoral theology in general.[20] Through his books, reviews
and articles, he brought out clearly the need for the practical application of theology. By "practical" he meant the
shepherding aspect of the ministry, namely, caring, guiding, healing, and sustaining. Schleiermacher did not un-

dertake any extensive writings on how practical theology in general, nor practical theology for the sick in particular, ought to be undertaken. Since the writings of Schleiermacher, much literature on the subject has appeared, of which only a few samples are cited in the following pages. J.J. Van Oosterzee[21] followed the principles of Schleiermacher. A variation of Schleiermacher's school is represented by the works of John G. Mackenzie. Mackenzie's view, and that of others who follow him, called for a dynamic relationship between psychology and theology.[22] His approach was not one of integration; instead, he appeared to have put emphasis on psychology rather than theology. He probably favoured the division between body, soul and mind. By the turn of the century, three authors seemed to have tackled the problem of pastoral care for the sick head on: Frank Lake, Robert A. Lambourne and Paul Tournier.

Frank Lake's voluminous book entitled Clinical Theology reflects his concern and interest in the contribution of theology to the care of the sick. In fact, the book resulted from seminars that he organized for the clergy in order to equip them to minister effectively to the sick. He was dealing primarily with pastoral care to the mentally ill. He did seem to favour a humanistic psychological model of healing of the sick.

Robert Lambourne's approach seems to draw on church traditions. His emphasis is the role of the (christian)

community in the process of treatment of the sick. He is
of the opinion that the christian community is not only
vital in itself but can use the traditional resources of
the sacraments, worship, koinonia in the healing process.
His book, Community, Church and Healing[23] brings out some
of his views.

Paul Tournier represents the holistic approach. He
sees in sickness more than a body to be x-rayed, operated
on and analyzed by laboratories. While he sees the value
of drugs or medicine for the sick, his emphasis is on the
meaning of sickness.[24]

Finally, it is important to look at the pastoral care
of the sick in North America around the turn of the century
in the Reformed tradition. Emphasis here, as in the other
sections, is briefly to survey and bring out the salient
principles and practices. A detailed discussion is not
intended here.

By the turn of this century, the church had conceded
not only to the language of science and popular ideas, but
to the appropriation of them into christian theology in
general, and pastoral care in particular. The liberal
culture (influenced greatly by scientific discoveries of
social science, economic prosperity and the breakdown of
the morals of christian culture) gradually but steadily
absorbed the christian foundation of pastoral theology to
the disadvantage of christian theology of pastoral care.

One of the first groups in the christian church to adopt modern psychology into official christian teaching about the cure of souls was the Emmanual Movement in Boston in 1905. Their official journal, Psychotherapy, literally "the healing of souls", carried articles by theologians influenced by psychology, by Freudian materials, and by medical and other psychological findings. Their primary aim was "the application of psychological principles to the problems of religion."[25] According to proponents of the Emmanual Movement, every minister practiced "psycho-therapy" consciously or unconsciously. By psychotherapy, the proponents meant clinical or scientific psychotherapy. They were of the opinion that it was time for the guidance of souls to be informed by the sciences rather than by tradition. Though the Emmanual Movement was short lived historically, it turned christian thought to the science of psychology. The medical practitioners resented or did not know what to do with the clergy. Some openly denied them access to their patients. Where ministers were not refused access, they (ministers) were told "to limit themselves to moral education. They almost had agreed to transform the care of souls into a branch of medicine and to work as physicians' aides."[26] According to Brooks Holifield, other events that contributed to the greater influence of psy-chology in America were the World Wars, especially the First World War. The war

introduced the masses to psychology, but it was
the reaction against the society that had gone to
war, that transformed psychologists and analysts
into symbols of cultural freedom.[27]

Hence psychology, taking the place of christian theology of

pastoral care to the sick, was not only an impetus to re-

bellion but also "offered a scientific means of success and

wisdom."[28]

The names of personologists, behaviourists, and psy-

choanalysts like Rogers, Skinner and Freud became household

names. The public was flooded with different types of

self-help books on psychology. The situation appeared

unredeemable for the church because of the low educational

standards of the ministers, especially in the Protestant

churches in America, perhaps the whole of North America.

As a response to the loss of an effective ministry of

pastoral care to the sick, pastors started to imitate doc-

tors, psychologists, psychiatrists, psychoanalysts and

social workers. Unfortunately, they could neither be com-

petent nor experts in these roles as they were not trained

for them. They tried as hard as they could to be what they

were not trained to be, and in the process, lost their own

identity and resources. One of these lost resources was

that of ritual. Throughout the history of the church,

especially in times of crisis such as sickness, As cor-

rectly pointed out by Clebsch and Jaekle, "pastoral ritual

diminishes, pastoral authority proportionately wanes."[29]

By the turn of the century much of the Protestant

christian church in America and possibly in Europe had

unfortunately abandoned ritualism for rationalism. The

result of the intermingling of christian pastoral care with

other helping professionals is best summarized by Clebsch

and Jaekle:

> Healing stands in great confusion because non-
> pastoral healing professions have learned both to
> encompass[30] and to outstrip pastoral methods of
> healing.

A medical practitioner's testimony of what his training was

like during this period summarizes the apparent conflict

and mutual disregard between medicine and theology. He

writes,

> Let me confess that early in our training my
> generation of physicians turned away from the
> religious aspect of life. At that time we were
> faced with fascinating series of intellectual
> problems for which concrete answers had to be
> found. The mystery of human illness and disease
> seemed to demand a diagnosis on factual rather
> than on a theoretical or spiritual level. The
> scientific spirit engulfed the medical student,
> it left little, if any,[31] time or inclination for
> religious contemplation.

The testimony of this medical practitioner typifies and

exemplifies the attitude of doctors to the clergy by the

turn of the century.

As a response to this type of attitude, the church's

ministry of healing took a form of quasi-religious psychol-

ogy. In some of the seminaries, pastoral theology became

pastoral psychology. The titles of such books as The Minister as a Diagnostician by Pruyser or a variation of such titles became popular. There emerged four approaches to pastoral theology especially to the sick.

The first school, represented by Thomas Oden and Wayne Oates, maintained that the church should do its ministry of healing from its own christian tradition. Thomas Oden's and Wayne Oates' school calls for pastoral theology to return to its basics:

> The task that lies ahead is the development of a post-modern, post-Freudian, neo-classical approach to christian pastoral care, which has taken seriously the resources of modernity, but which has also penetrated its illusions, and having found the best of modern psychotherapies still problematic, has turned again to classical tradition for its bearings, yet without disavowing what it has learnt from modern clinical experience.[32]

The second school represented by Carrol Wise[33] and Paul E. Johnson sought a marriage between theology and psychology.[34] However, it was not an equal partnership. Psychology for this school dictates to theology the terms of the marriage. Wise dropped the term, pastoral counseling, in favour of pastoral psychotherapy. As to what is the difference between pastoral psychotherapy and the other secular psychotherapies, Wise responds, the difference is in the practitioner. It is obvious that even if such dualistic orientation (theology and psychotherapy) worked for Wise, it would not work for most pastors without Wise's background in personology. Nonetheless Wise left a legacy to pastoral theology.

Charles Gerkin makes an important observation on

Wise's legacy:

> The style an ethos of clinical education for
> ministry strongly supported the model of integra-
> tion made explicit by Carrol Wise and Paul John-
> son. The person of the pastoral care trainee
> became the focus of attention. Did the pastor in
> his or her person evidence the integration of
> biblical and theological images of ministry with
> psychological savvy and expertise? This became
> the central training issue.[35]

It certainly does not reflect the sit-im-leben of its

founder Anton Boison, and his legacy to the church in the

ministry to the sick via the approach of the Clinical Pas-

toral Education, popularly abbreviated C.P.E. For Anton

Boison, the founder of the C.P.E. movement, psychology was

not to replace theology. For him, the major concern was

how theology could be made relevant by learning from the

data of the living document, as he termed the persons to

whom ministry was offered. Charles Gerkin correctly points

out

> in his later years, he was highly critical of the
> involvement of his followers in psychoanalysis
> and secular psychotherapy. For Boison the care
> of souls had to do fundamentally with the raw
> stuff of religious experience.[36]

Religion, and for that matter christian theology of pastor-

al care, should be a partner with the other disciplines,

including psychology. Among the literature of the current

period, the writing of Charles Gerkin reflects the concern

of Anton Boison on the need for an integrated approach in

order to offer holistic healing to the sick.

The third school of the dualistic problem is represented by Howard Clinebell whose book Basic Types of Pastoral Counselling became a standard text in many seminaries.
His approach was a break from Wise's and Johnson's school
and was also different from Thomas Oden's. Clinebell advo-
cates an eclectic approach.[37] He suggests that pastoral
theology should absorb some of the therapeutic approaches
that enhance psychological growth.

The fourth school is that of the Hiltnerian Model.
According to this approach, pastoral theology is only the
shepherding aspect of christian theology and must neither
be allowed to dominate it nor be absorbed by other aspects
of christian theology, or even worse, by other disciplines.
In ministering to people in need, pastoral theology must be
opened to the sciences of personality but must not be absorbed by it.[38] However, some insights from the sciences
can and do influence christian theology and cause it to
respond. In short, this is the Praxis/reflection model or
what Schleiermacher called Hermeneutic Circle. Its foundation should always remain in the christian tradition and
never by uprooted from it. The models of North American
pastoral theology, presently, especially pastoral care to
the sick, trace their roots to any one or combination of
these schools. The Clinical Movement challenged the
church's ministry to the sick and it inevitably exhibits
some form from these schools.

However, in some of the training centres and in available literature, the resources for identity and function predominantly come from the resources of the christian tradition. Psychology is relevant but not dominant. It seems C.P.E. is also affecting even the scientific treatment of people who are sick. This is evidenced in the increase in grants for the employment and training of chaplains and renewed interest on the part of governments for the presence of the church in most institutions. Finally, it is reflected by including clinical training in the syllabi of seminaries. It is also a predominant model of the christian pastoral theology for the sick in North America in this century.

To conclude this chapter,[39] the relationship of theology and psychology is maturing to a level of mutual respect for equals and indicates that the scale swings in favour of theology again in North America. Perhaps this may be reflecting the spiritual quest of the West. After a long search, the West may have come full circle.

Footnotes

[1]Wayne Oates, New Dimension in Pastoral Care (Philadelphia: Fortress Press, 1970), p. 3.

[2]Ibid.

[3]William A. Clebsch and Charles R. Jaekle, Pastoral Care in Historical Perspective (Englewood Cliffs, New Jersey: Prentice-Hall Inc., 1964), p. 11.

[4]Richard H. Niebuhr and David D. Williams (eds.), The Ministry in Historical Perspectives (New York: Harper and Brothers, 1956) for more detailed information.

[5]Walker Willston, A History of the Christian Church, revised by C.C. Richardson, W. Panck and R.T. Handy (New York: Charles Scribner and Sons, 1959) for more detailed information.

[6]William A. Clebsch and Charles R. Jaekle, Pastoral Care in Historical Perspective, p. 15.

[7]John McNeil, A History of the Care of Souls (New York: Harper and Row Publishers, 1951), p. 101.

[8]Ibid.

[9]Clebsch and Jaekle, Pastoral Care in Historical Perspective, p. 20.

[10]Charles Norris Cochrane, Christianity and Classical Culture (New York: Oxford University Press, 1944).

[11]John McNeil, A History of the Care of Souls, p. 24.

[12]Clebsch and Jaekle, Pastoral Care in Historical Perspective, p. 24.

[13]Bishop Bunchard, Corrector et Medius: Medieval Handbooks of Pennance, trans. John J. McNeil and Helena M. Cramer (New York: Columbia University Press, 1938), p. 323-345.

[14]Disciplinary Decrees of the General Council, the Fourth Lateran Council Canons 21-22, trans. and commentary by J. Schroeder (St. Louis B. Herider Co., 1937), p. 260.

[15] Joseph Martos, Doors to the Sacred (New York: Image Books, 1982), p. 29.

[16] Martin E. Marty, Health and Medicine in the Lutheran Tradition, (Crossword, NY, 1983).

[17] John McNeil, History of the Care of Souls, pp. 192-193.

[18] Ibid.

[19] Martin Luther King, Jr. (source unknown).

[20] Friederich Schleriermacher, Brief Outline on the Study of Theology, trans. Torrence N. Tice (Richmond: John Knox, 1966).

[21] J.J. Van Oosterzee, Practical Theology (New York: Scribners' Sons, 1899).

[22] John A. Mackenzie, Souls in the Making: An Introduction to Pastoral Psychology (New York: Macmillan, 1929).

[23] R.A. Lambourne, Community Church and Healing: A Study of Some Corporate Aspects of the Church's Ministry to the Sick (London: Darton Longman and Todd, 1963).

[24] Paul Tournier, Four Best Books in One Volume (New York: Iverson-Norman, 1977).

[25] E. Brooks Hollifield, A History of Pastoral Care in America: From Salvation to Self Realization (Nashville: Abingdon Press, 1983), p. 202.

[26] Ibid.

[27] Ibid.

[28] Ibid.

[29] Clebsch and Jaekle, Pastoral Care in Historical Perspective, p. 68.

[30] Ibid.

[31] Howard M. Kravetz, "Illness and Religion: A Physician's Testimony", Journal of Pastoral Care 12 (1958): 174-175.

[32] Thomas Oden, "Rediscovering Lost Identity", Journal of Pastoral Care 34(5) (March 1980).

[33]Carrol Wise, The Meaning of Pastoral Care (New York: Harper and Row Publishers, 1966).

[34]Paul E. Johnson, Psychology of Pastoral Care: The Pastoral Ministry in Theory and Practice (Nashville: Abingdon Press, 1953).

[35]Charles V. Gerkin, "Revisioning: Pastoral Counselling in a Hermeneutic Mode", The Living Human Document (Nashville: Abingdon Press, 1984), p. 26.

[36]Ibid., p. 38.

[37]Howard Clinebell, Basic Types of Pastoral Counselling (Nashville: Abingdon Press, 1982).

[38]Seward Hiltner, Preface to Pastoral Theology (Nashville: Abingdon Press, 1958).

[39]The writing of this chapter has been frustrating. The library resources on pastoral care to the sick in the Reformed tradition are scarce. I wondered whether that reflects the enigmatic nature of the shepherding aspect of the ministry or the lack thereof in writing, specific approaches to the sick in the Reformed tradition, especially the Presbyterian tradition.

Pictorial Summation of Thesis

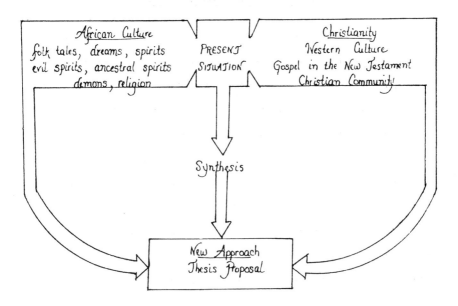

African Culture
folk tales, dreams, spirits
evil spirits, ancestral spirits
demons, religion

PRESENT
SITUATION

Christianity
Western Culture
Gospel in the New Testament
Christian Community

Synthesis

New Approach
Thesis Proposal

5. AN APPROACH TO AFRICAN CHRISTIAN

PASTORAL CARE FOR THE SICK

In the previous chapters, the attempt has been to provide a background to what follows in this chapter. In the exploration of the principles and practices of pastoral care in the West, especially in the Reformed tradition, four schools have emerged. In each of these schools, the various authors have tried to make the ministry of healing relevant to those in need. An area of tension in these schools has been how to integrate the ministry of healing with the psycho-social and cultural milieu of the sick. To what extent the psycho-social and cultural aspect will influence the theology of the christian ministry of healing is a constant conflict.

What is certain is that there is the need for integration. Any one individual is a product of a culture. In other words, each of us perceives and interprets meaning with symbols and signs from a certain cultural perspective. Pastoral theology in general, and for that matter pastoral care, should engage in "grubbing in the root systems of human need",[1] or what Anton Boison called studying the "living document". What Hiltner suggests about theological studies in general is true of christian pastoral care in Africa in particular:

> All realms of theological inquiry involve a rela-
> tionship between faith and culture. Sometimes

the questions raised in culture--for example,
what kind of stability can man have in a world of
instability?--can be answered by faith.[2]

For Hiltner then, "faith can remain faithful and relevant
only when it is in constant and discriminating dialogue
with culture."[3] However, there must not only be a dialogue, but the dialogue must be dialectic. Christian pastoral theology is not simply a matter of applying principles of pastoral care taken from another situation, or just
applying some Biblical or christian doctrines to the African situation.

As indicated by Clebsch and Jaekle,

Throughout its history, christian pastoral care
has borrowed from the societies in which it lived
and has adapted to its pastoral use, various
theories of the human soul.[4]

There is, however, a difference between the view above and
the one intended or pursued in this thesis. The one intended is not an eclectic model such as Clinebell's; the
approach intended combines theological and cultural exege-
sis. It is an approach whereby one digs deep into the
symbols of a culture to determine the commonalities or
differences in christian theology of pastoral care. The
commonalities arise out of a deeper search in both. It is
not pick and choose. It does not insist that christian
theology manufactured in some other cultural milieu should
fit into an African situation, nor does it insist that
christian theology should give up its unique claims to

African culture. Consequently, the approaches of the four

schools of pastoral care are not applicable directly to the

African situation. That is not to suggest that they do not

have any contributions to make, for African christian the-

ology of pastoral care for the sick should not be a wholly

imported theology. African christian theology must be

produced with African materials even though substantially

christian theology is universal. But christian theology is

universal only when it can be particular. In short, it

must be a process of evolution, not a program to which one

adheres. Any christian theology of pastoral care to the

sick is only a part of the christian theology. Therefore,

the words of Masamba Ma Mpollo, are imperative for pastoral

theology:

> In Africa, pastoral psychology and pastoral care
> cannot be studied and developed outside the
> emerging African theology, which is an attempt to
> interpret the Biblical message using the catego-
> ries, symbols and psychosocial, cultural[5] and
> political structures of the African peoples.

In this endeavor, scholars of christian theology should be

warned of the

> contradictions in African identity resulting from
> cultural ambiguities, the christian and colonial
> history of oppression, the repression of African
> cultures and their systems of health and healing
> situations still found in many alien forms of
> pastoral [6] care practiced by some African
> churches.

In this attempt to adumbrate African christian theology of

pastoral care to the sick, it is imperative to begin with

African culture and look at the theme of divination.

The mechanics of divination, who and how one becomes a diviner have already been discussed in Chapter Three and need no repetition here. It is only the deductive type that is of concern here. As indicated earlier, the task of the diviner is "to scrutinize the past in order to identify the spiritual and human agents responsible for the human and communal misfortune."[7] The function of the diviner in African society cannot be over-emphasized. One should look at divining as an active listening phenomenon.

From the discussion of who and how one becomes a diviner, it is appropriate to suggest that christian ministers/priests in Africa can be justifiably called diviners. In fact, the word Osofo in Akan applied to the christian ministers, connotes a form of divination.

The diviner of Ghanaian society can be likened to the Greek god Hermes. His function was one of "transmuting what is beyond human understanding into a form that human intelligence can grasp."[8] Christians who are sick in Ghana approach the christian diviner exhibiting almost the same attitude that people expected of the Greek god Hermes. The desire to comprehend mysteries of life (of which sickness is a part) is almost innate and universal. Such a desire or logical quest is almost inevitable when one falls sick. It is a search for meaning.

The christian diviner therefore has a task of relating the language of the pain expressed through the symbols of

the church to that of the good news of Christ Jesus. Like
Hermes, he or she is a carrier of that good message and is
expected to help the sick find meaning in the gospel in the
affliction or pain.

Some metaphors in the field of pastoral care that are
used to describe human beings are the "living document" and
the "palm kernel". If the life in a palm nut kernel is
hampered, most probably it may be traced to the nut. Relief calls for someone sensitive and knowledgeable to carry
out the arduous task of peeling off the many layers until
the seed is reached. The process of uncovering the kernel
patiently, attentively and with skill can be likened to
deductive divining or active listening to a troubled soul
or sick person. As suggested by Richard Yadeau,

> the patient is not a disease entity or medical
> problem to be treated with surgery, radiation or
> chemotherapy, healing is a process of profound
> dimensions, involving virtually all aspects of a
> person's life--physical, spiritual, psychologi-
> cal, social dimensions, environmental and even
> political.[9]

Therefore, the christian diviner's model for ministry
to the sick is not the same as the medical model which is
"end-goal" oriented and can be summarized as a linear process from information gathering to compilation and evalua-
tion of information gathered to tentative diagnosis to
referral to approved therapies for the condition diagnosed
to choice to prescription for treatment and finally to
actual treatment. The end-goal of the medical consultation

is thus something apart from the personalities of either patient or physician. In the pastoral model, "the goal and the process are one". The treatment in pastoral care be-gins with the initiation of the relationship between pa-tient and healer and continues through the relationship. Thus, in a desirable African approach, the eliciting of information by the healer is itself part of the healing process especially when it is carried out empathetically. As the sensitive religious therapist poses his/her ques-tions, the displaced pieces of the Rubik Cube begin to fall into place in the minds of the hearers. In some cases, the treatment prescribed at the end of the process is almost irrelevant and a placebo. The healing has already started and advanced toward its conclusion.

The christian diviner then must be a "listener of stories" if he is to be an effective care giver. This point is well articulated by Charles Gerkin:

> Pastoral counsellors are, more than anything else, listeners to and interpretors of stories. Persons seek out a pastoral counsellor because they need someone to listen to their story. Most often the story is tangled, it involves themes, plots, and counterplots. The story itself is, of course, an interpretation of experience. To seek counselling usually means that the interpretation has become painful, the emotions evoked by the interpretation powerful and conflicted.[10]

In the above quotation, the words "counsellor" could be replaced by "diviner", and "interpretation" by "divina-tion". In pastoral care, one would like to see the sick reinterpret their stories themselves rather than christian diviners doing it for them. The stories sick Africans bring to the diviner are every day stories. They are also expressed in every day language. The stories normally center around relationships affecting one's clan. The symbols and signs used to express these relationships come also from the every day life situations of the cultural milieu.

In the Ghanaian situation, one might assume that both the sick and the christian diviner share a common language, so that there is no linguistic barrier to overcome. However, that assumption can lead to inattentive listening. For the sick, the language of pain and strong emotion is a very important, if not the important part of the story. The christian diviner should therefore seek for clarification of any symbols, signs and images used, for as further suggested by Gerkin; "for humans it is impossible to separate experience from language."[11] Moreover, meanings derived from experience are mostly subjective; therefore, it is only the sick who can best reinterpret their experiences with less pain and resolved emotion, thus deriving meaningful insight and giving the sick strength, hope and faith.

The christian diviner's task then is a process in which he seeks to enable the christians who fall sick to interpret their life experiences within their understanding of the Christ event and its significance for their lives.

It must avoid projection or imposition, or taking over the interpretation; it is the enabling quality of the diviner's ministry that allows the sick to drink from the well of living water expressed in all christian resources. This calls for suspension of judgement on the part of the christian diviner. It calls for an unconditional acceptance, openness, and unqualified trust. Thus the Grace of God is concretized in a life situation; the love of God incarnated in the christian diviner and a process of healing of the most holistic kind is begun. The Son of God becomes the Son of humankind. It is reaffirming in a concrete way the traditional teaching that Christ became a human being and "dwelt among us" (John 1:4) as in the healing of Zacchaeus (Luke 19) and the woman at the well (John 4). Among other things said about the healings of Jesus, Morris Maddock suggests that

> His [Jesus'] healings found their origin in the essential nature of God and were a direct expression of his incarnation. He loved people—he was the human expression of the divine love of God for his creation. 'God so loved the world...' (John 3:16a), and was utterly caring and compassionate. His healings followed naturally from a nature that was essentially compassionate.[12]

The African christian diviner has many resources from which to draw. But the diviner's primary resources are the christian resources expressed in the ministry of Jesus. For as Maddock summarizes aptly, "It is in the healing ministry of Jesus that we see the love of God incarnate, the word became flesh, full of grace and truth."[13] The christian diviner also has to take the notion and function of the traditional diviner seriously. The christian diviner becomes an agent for the task of healing by the interpretation and integration of christian theology and African culture. This is how one inaugurates the kingdom of God by signs in the pattern of Jesus Christ, who inaugurated the kingdom of God through his ministry of healing among other ministries (Matt. XII:28).

The christian diviner must also point people beyond themselves. It is not sufficient to listen actively only. The christian diviner should go beyond that to enable the sick to come to some insights. For the christian diviner, active listening must seek to give meaning to sickness theologically. The christian diviner's identity is theological and must be an indispensable factor in the caring for the sick. In short, every period of active listening must aim at bringing a healthy appropriation of the love of God and a sense of gratitude to Him who is the creator and sustainer. It should evoke a renewal of commitment to a deeper sense of stewardship in life and creation as a whole. All this must come from experiencing the diviner's personhood rather than just hearing words. There are some very important themes on which the christian diviner should concentrate in divining with African christians who are sick. These themes are inextricably related to sickness in the world view of most Africans and are an integral part of their ethos. These themes are: a) witchery; b) sin and sickness; and c) implication of the rituals of sacrifice and eating for the sick and their community.

The christian diviner caring for the sick in Africa cannot and should not dismiss cases or allegations of witchery as pagan and suspicious. The witchery phenomenon is an important part of African cosmology and reality; it is a more frequent concern of those sick and hence should be an integral part of christian pastoral care to the sick. In the case of the bewitched or allegedly bewitched sick, the christian diviner's task goes beyond the individual concern. As the stories unfold, some unresolved conflict, misunderstandings, or grudges are disclosed. The unresolved conflict may be with the immediate parties or with past generations. The conflict may have arisen from or been precipitated by some inappropriate word or deed of the suspected witch. Once the hurt has been caused or perceived to be caused, the maxim that time is a great healer is not applicable. Indeed, as other misfortunes follow, the hurt gets deeper, and the thought of being under the control of someone is confirmed. Incidents that confirm such thoughts are many. They can arise from illness (especially during the farming and fishing seasons), unsuccessful projects, whether individual or communal, sudden severe illness, and prolonged sickness. The christian diviner may, in the process of exploring with the sick, invite the family of the alleged witch. It is these cases in which sickness and healing will involve other families or even a whole community in some cases. At this stage, the community resources can be brought in, and the christian diviner may at this stage seek primarily to be a facilitator in the healing process which usually involves verbalized confession, forgiveness and reconciliation. The christian ministry of healing can be represented here covertly and overtly. It may also be kerygmatic to the whole community. As will be pointed out later, healing, forgiveness and reconciliation go on in the community, but for the christian who is sick and part of this scenario, it must be borne in mind that whatever goes on in the ministry of healing is only the reactment or application of what Christ, the first ancestor, accomplished and commanded His followers to do likewise. Thus is enacted the fulfillment of the wish of Jesus in Beatitude: "Blessed are those who hunger and thirst for righteousness, Blessed are the merciful, Blessed are the pure in heart, Blessed are the peacemakers. You are the salt of the earth" (Matt. 5:6, 7, 8, 9, 13). There is also a fulfillment of the Lord's Prayer, "Thy kingdom come, thy will be done on earth as it is in heaven" (Matt. 6:10).

There are many ways of looking at witchery in times of sickness. For the christian diviner, it calls to question

Jesus as the Christ. In other words, it is a christological question and a christological response is sought. Be-
neath these questions are how the sick person understands
and believes Jesus as "Son of Man" and "Son of God", as
his/her "Lord and Saviour", as his/her "healer and redeemer". The christians who are sick have used all these in
worship and in daily life to some extent and are now trying
to understand or reinterpret them in times of sickness.
Many sick people at their bedside, or at their shrines, in
their homes, ask some very fundamental questions of their
belief. Such fundamental questions include: If Jesus
healed the sick in his day, why does He not heal me now?
If, as the pastors say, God is powerful and cares for and
loves me, why does God not free me from the power of these
witches? It is in these moments that the familiar beliefs
in the power of the ancestors to free the bewitched and to
punish the witch are most prevalent. From this perspective, the theological healing in some cases in Africa takes
precedence over or is as important as scientific medicine
to the sick.

Underlying such questions is the need on the part of
christians who are sick for a more immediately relevant
incarnational christology expressed in familiar terms. In
response to this call, some African theologians have attempted christologies such as Jesus as ancestor, senior
brother, and even as witch doctor. These metaphors ob-

viously have a meaningful concreteness to which the sick can relate. It is only appropriate then to examine briefly these more popular christological themes and their implications for the christians who are sick in Africa.

For Africans, the first ancestor is the founder of the tribe, clan and family; in some cases, even the individual, as Ghanaians believe in the reincarnation of the spirit of an ancestor in later generations. The term "first ancestor" has its roots and connotation in John 1:1, 14, and the concept of the "Son of Man" in Mk. 1:13, 3:33-34. For many Africans, the concept of the humanity of Jesus is most helpful in times of crisis associated with witchery. The stories of Jesus casting out demons are often meditated upon as Africans perceive themselves to be in similar states as those whom Jesus healed.

The thought of Jesus as a first ancestor is also inspired or supported by many anthropomorphisms in the Old Testament as well as by the similarity between Ghanaian cosmology and New Testament cosmology. In times of sickness, the sick want to experience Jesus as an ancestor. The Lord's prayer is appropriated in a new and perhaps a deeper dimension. If Jesus is seen as a first ancestor, the implication for freeing the sick from witches is greater. The sick christians do not, therefore, feel that they are with an abstract saviour, they are called upon to believe. They are ready to believe because a first ancestor,

Jesus, died to free them, heal them and accept them at death into the community of saints. Consequently, the promises of Jesus can be fully trusted. Some popular Biblical statements of Jesus that are recommended and recited most often include the following: "I have come that they may have life and have it more abundantly" in John 10:10; the concept of a "good shepherd" in Peter 2:25; "the gate", the "owner", the good news, of Jesus triumphing over principalities and powers of evil in Mark 3:23ff. The notion of Jesus as a second Adam is also open to viewing Jesus as a spiritual first ancestor of christians.

Other scholars like Aylward Shorter prefer to liken the healing role of Jesus to witch doctoring. For Shorter, Jesus was a "healer-exorcist". Shorter wants christians to "view Jesus healing people as a means of inaugurating the kingdom or reign of God".[14] While these attempts are laudable, they raise some fundamental christological questions. Should every sickness of christians be healed before they can say that Jesus is truly a saviour, redeemer, Lord? The answer is an emphatic no. All these are but attempts to provide different models to appropriate the Christ event in times of crisis.

Theologically, it must be emphasized that to say that one is saved by Christ only means that one's life in health and in sickness, in hopes and in doubts, in joys and in sorrows is mediated through Christ so that one can participate in the love of God, which gives meaning to all existence. It does not guarantee problem-proof and sickness-free life. Hence, these pastoral models are to be used to enhance, encourage and nurture faith and to deepen commitment. They are attempts to reinterpret stories, derive appropriate meanings, and widen experience of the love of God in Christ. The New Testament does give christians, particularly those in the ministry of healing, models to emulate. If Christ is to be "Lord of all", if all creation, all conditions of life, all "principalities and powers" are to bow at the name of Jesus, then christian diviners have the task to use all the signs and symbols through which African christians can believe, feel and experience. One that can be used effectively is the rite of anointing the sick.

The christian diviner has to transpose christian signs and symbols as part of a total package of pastoral care. One such symbol long unrecognized and forgotten in some of the Reformed churches, especially the Presbyterian tradition, is the rite of anointing the sick. It is unfortunate that the reformed tradition, especially the Presbyterian tradition, did not separate the abuses and overuses of this symbol from its proper use. One doubts whether the word "sacrament" should still be limited only to those rites which Jesus personally performed in His time. For Presbyterians in Africa, this rite of anointing the sick can be incorporated in the theology and practice of pastoral care. Rituals are an integral part of the practice of the traditional healer/priest and African life as a whole. It is therefore a matter of common sense that the christian healer incorporates it. It is not adopting for adopting's sake. Anointing is a powerful means of care, it is found in both the christian and African heritage and offers the sick spiritual nurture and healing. The christian diviners do not necessarily have to believe or teach that the oil has a power by itself to effect healing. Like the Eucharist, it is a means of grace. God, by His grace, could effect healing by the laying of hand, by use of oil, bread, water and wine. Like the ministers who preach, christian diviners have nothing in themselves to effect a change of heart. It is the work of God's spirit using their words to convince, correct and exhort. One cannot see why such a logic cannot be applied to the rite of anointing the sick with oil.

As indicated earlier, in times of sickness the African christian, like any other person, asks questions which cannot be empirically, logically or scientifically answered. Such questions may appear to be philosophical, but in actuality no philosophical answers are needed. Sickness at some stages is a mystery. It is doubtful if there is any theological or biblical or homilectical explanation that can answer without an iota of doubt the questions asked.

Why am I sick? Why am I sick now?... The responses to
these questions are best given in rituals, such as anointing, and the Eucharist through which the christians who are
sick may find meaning.

Life is both physical and spiritual. Sickness is also
physical and spiritual. Sickness destabilizes the equilibrium between the living and the dead, the sacred and secular. Therefore, it is a matter of necessity to restore
that balance, peace, stability, equilibrium, and health by
other symbolic agents. Oil is popular in traditional use
for healing in Africa as elsewhere so the cultural context
is already provided for oil; the sacrament of anointing
with oil is intended to show that, for christians, neither
sickness nor death need be feared. Christians are encouraged to face these boldly and live through them, not try to
escape. For through this ritual, the love of God in Christ
may be a source of strength for them. In the ritual of
anointing, the christians renew their belief in the death
and resurrection of Christ. The smooth flow of oil is a
sign of the smooth flow of God's love and grace reaching
the sick, when physical abilities are incapacitating.

LAYING OF HANDS AND PUBLIC PRAYER

Another aspect of the healing ministry that needs
mentioning is the laying on of hands. In a culture where
touching has much significance, the act of laying hands

could be included in the ministry of healing to the sick. In the Presbyterian tradition, it is used only for ordination, as a sign of being set apart. However, it could be included in healing as well, for in African culture there is hardly any treatment that is not followed by the laying on of hands. It does not mean that the hands have some power to heal. The warmth of a touch from a christian diviner will convey a sense of care and empathy. It is true though that it has been over used and abused by the electronic church in the West and itinerant freelance Evangelists and leaders of the independent African churches. But, that is not sufficient ground for other christians to ignore a vital tool for healing. Even the reason that the Reformed tradition as a whole did not fully adopt it into its pastoral life does not mean it cannot or should not be used in Africa if it is helpful. If one truly believes that the wind blows where it wills (i.e., the spirit of God cannot be limited), that belief is negated by condemning the laying on of hands. Surely God's healing power can be effected on the act of laying hands with prayer by the elders. If the church is to offer total healing to African christians in times of sickness, one cannot afford to be selective for reasons of misuse, over use, tradition, biases, or even individual fears. It must be borne in mind that it is Christ who heals and members of his church are only agents. It must also be borne in mind that rituals are an important aspect of life in Africa. Indeed, life is a procession of sacraments. Every stage and condition of life is marked by some form of sacrament. By sacrament is meant here the definition of Theodore of Mopsuestia as quoted by Joseph Martos that, "every sacrament points to invisible and ineffable realities by means of signs and symbols."[15]

A CHANGE IN TRADITIONAL PASTORAL LANGUAGE

A new approach also calls for a change of language in the care of the sick. In fact, one would propose that in the shrines, homes, hospitals, or wherever the sick are visited, traditional christian language such as "pray about it", "read your Bible" and "Let us pray", should be replaced. To some African christians, these phrases sound abstract and academic. African expressions are not only appropriate, but should be encouraged so that christian diviners use phrases such as "Let us divine in the word of God", when they mean "Let us read the scriptures". "Do divine with the Lord" should replace "pray about it". It is important in the light of the African culture that the traditional christian theology in general, and pastoral care in particular, should be transposed into new symbols and signs. This approach will not only help to make the gospel more meaningful, but will also evoke powerful spirituality which is a necessary ingredient to a christian ministry of healing.

THE RELATIONSHIP BETWEEN SIN AND SICKNESS

The question of the relationship between sin and sickness seems to be as old as humanity. In almost every culture this relationship underlies any attempt to care for the sick. All religions have tried and are trying to understand, teach and explain this relationship to its adherents. The Judeo-christian faith is no exception.

In the Old Testament, some passages suggest that it is God who willed sickness (Deut. 29:22; 2 Chron. 21:18-19). There is also an explicit belief that God heals sickness at times by God's forgiveness (Psalm 103; Hosea 7:1). The writer of the book of Judges abounds in such examples. In some cases the sin of the individual is said to effect the whole community (Deut. 5:9; Jer. 31:29; Ezek. 18:2; Josh. 7:24). In his ministry, Jesus attributed some sickness to the sin of the individual (the healing of the paralytic, Mt. 9:1-8; Mk. 2:12; Lk. 5:7-26).

It is obvious from these examples that the relationship between sin and sickness is complex. It cannot be over-simplified as caused solely by sin or solely by external agents. This profound and complex paradox or even mystery raises very fundamental questions, such as what causes which? Which depends on the other? When does the solution of one automatically cover the other? It is even more complex in an undifferentiated society such as Ghana.

The christian diviner has to take each case on its own terms. An active listening approach to one person is different from the approach of another person. In most pastoral encounters, there are implicit and explicit confessions made. It is these confessions that will dictate the pastoral direction. But in christian pastoral theology, the love of God in Christ is fundamental. If sin is seen as an alienation or estrangement from oneself, the family, society, and fear or anxiety of alienation from God is even more detrimental. The question, "Who am I?" fills the thoughts of the sick. The sense of dependence on the ultimate God is implicit or explicit in prayer, song or even in screams and sighs. The notion of sickness as a punishment frequently pervades the thoughts of the sick. Even among educated christians some of these thoughts are aroused during the meditations when literal applications of the Bible suggest themselves.

The first principle for an open confession, questioning and sharing of doubts, is in the example of Jesus. For Jesus, the value of a person is supreme. Forgiveness for sin is important. Faith is an instrument to heal mind, body and soul. For Jesus, morals are important, but secondary. The most important factor is the person and his/her search to encounter God's love afresh or to renew a past encounter. The "why" of the sick is answered best by the "how" of God's love for them while they were yet sinners (Rom. 5:5). They can now depend on Grace rather than on legal codes which only increase the guilt and sense of failure.

The christian diviner in Africa has to help the christian sick to come to a realization that his/her sickness is important to God, that God's love for him/her is not diminished, that the sickness by itself is a confession to God and God has granted forgiveness. It must also be pointed out that some space must be given to personal confession. There must be some space for the sick to express conflict or failure, both apparent or real. When, and if, there is a need for an extension of the reconciliation between the person and Christ to a member of the family of the sick, it should be encouraged. If some responsibility must be undertaken, that too should be encouraged. What must be emphasized however is that these things by themselves do not grant forgiveness. Instead, they result from the encounter of reconciliation with God through Christ. It is at this stage of the christian diviner's ministry that the Reformed doctrine of "Justification by faith through the spirit not by works" (Ephesians 2:1-9) is most appropriate.

It is hoped that this approach will produce the inner healing and provide strength to cope with the physical sickness. In some cases like those cited from Tournier and Appiah-Kubi, the sin aspect can cause the physical sickness. But in others, the christian diviner may help to put the sickness into some perspective, or provide tools to incorporate the sickness into his/her total life experience and reinterpret a new dynamic meaning. The word "dynamic" here means a new driving force with an enabling, strengthened spirit.

It is also hoped that this approach will encourage the African christian from feelings of obsession concerning obedience to every moral code. It should result in a sense of gratitude rather than of guilt. Fate becomes faith; doubts become courage; destiny becomes freedom. Life, inspired by hope, becomes a celebration of victories over failures, love over evil, hope in Christ who loves, cares, sustains, comforts and heals. All these are best confirmed in a ritual or Eucharist.

THE USE OF RITUALS IN PASTORAL CARE TO THE SICK

The Eucharist can be seen as a rite of intensification. In general, in Africa that is how sacrifices of expiation and propitiation are interpreted in the case of the sick.

In Africa, most rites are like openings to encounter the unseen powers. They are a means or opportunity for religious experience. In these experiences, one is lifted into another dimension of life in which one discovers a new and deeper meaning, or revives a lost meaning, especially

in the case of the sick. In Ghana, the sacrifices of expiation and propitiation, consumated in a meal, are aimed at
affirming and strengthening the bond of unity among the
members of the clan or tribe.

Reformed theology in general and the Calvinist tradition in particular, speaks of the sacraments (baptism and
communion) as "signs" and "seals". It is not the intention
here to go into details of the Reformed theology of the
sacrament. There are many volumes available to consult on
this topic. The intention is briefly to state only the
salient ideas and see how they can be interpreted into a
christian theology of pastoral care to African christians
who are sick.

For Calvin, the purpose of the sacrament was one of
"confirming and sealing the promise itself, and of making
it more evident to us, in a sense ratifying it."[16] The
strengthening aspect is primarily in the faith of the believers in the word of God. Perhaps, to explain what he
means by "promise", Calvin says that the sacraments (baptism and communion) are witnesses of the Grace of God and
"are like seals of the good will that He [God] feels toward
us, which by attesting that good will to us, sustain, nour-
ish, confirm, and increase our faith."[17] It must, however,
be cautioned that this does not mean that these signs and
seals have powers in themselves to perform miracles for
increasing faith. Their power to affect any healing is

tied to the power of God, through God's spirit. It is through the spirit "by whose power alone our hearts are penetrated and affections moved and our souls opened for the sacraments to enter in."[18]

For Calvin, the "signs" and "seals" are not just examples, illustrations, or even depictions.[19] The "signs and seals of God's promise" are to show clearly that God assures the person of His/Her divine commitment; that christian spiritually cleansed from sins as they outwardly wash in water and share fellowship in a candle-light dinner. These seals and signs express God's love and romance with His/Her people in order to enable God's people to realize their potentials to be truly children of God. Christians are called to faithful living and depending on the Grace of God. In light of the above understanding, the African christians who are sick need not approach communion with a sense of guilt for breaking tribal code, or for being bewitched or chased by an evil spirit. For God has promised in these "signs" and "seals" to sustain, guide, protect, heal and reconcile. Living is not an individual effort but a gratuitous response to God's promise. The sacrament of communion is inextricably connected with baptism. The promises of God were received first in baptism, so whatever is done in communion must be related to baptism in Reformed theology.

The sacrament of communion under discussion now has been called by five different names in the various traditions of the christian faith. In some cases, a few of the names are typical of the traditions, in other cases some names are used interchangeably within the same tradition. These names include: the mass or sacrament of the alter, the sacrament, communion, the Eucharist, and the Lord's Supper.

Each of these designations has some helpful pastoral care implication to christians in general, and those who are sick, in particular. One would therefore submit that the exclusive association of some of these names with the theological emphasis of some traditions is a luxury christian diviners in Africa should avoid.

It is difficult to trace the origin of the word "mass". There are also many discrepancies about its development. What is certain is that the word "mass" was discontinued in the Reformed tradition. In the Roman tradition it is used to emphasize the atoning sacrifice for the sin of humankind. No other sacrifice is either necessary or will meet the standard of God. All that human beings can do is to identify themselves with that offering and enjoy the benefits. In this theory, the humanity of Christ is emphasized. In the Roman Catholic tradition, the real presence is accentuated in the celebration. While one might object to the notion of the continuing sacrifice after resurrection and the notion of the real presence, nonetheless, the notion of the continuing work of redemption in this understanding is important for believers who are sick. The notion of redemption continuing enables christians to approach the mass with a belief that God continues to forgive sins when one comes in repentance. According to the Council of Trent, Christ, for these believers who are sick, is the "victim offered and the immolation in the sacramental order."[20]

When this act is referred to as THE sacrament, it does not deny the existence of other sacraments. For Protestants, such as the Presbyterians, it acknowledges baptism and for the Roman Catholics it acknowledges the other six sacraments. It emphasizes human wickedness and the finality of the victory of Jesus Christ, the victory of love over hatred, faith over fear, hope over despair. The notion of THE sacrament tries to show that what God has promised through the prophets, has now been concretely demonstrated before all eyes as witness to the believer. The greatest weakness of people is overcome; the power of God is shown forth. So the christian believers can approach God with their sickness boldly because the ultimate goal of God can never be defeated. It may be frustrated for a while, but victory is certain. It helps the christians who are sick to look beyond their sickness.

Eucharist is a transliteration from the Greek which can mean to gladden, cheer, rejoice, beseech, pray, connoting thanks, gratidude, appreciation. This understanding emphasizes and symbolizes the act or event as the gift of God, i.e., Grace. God is gracious to humankind; God gives life and enables human beings to live that life in any circumstances. In the notion of Eucharist, humanity is reminded of its weaknesses and called to struggle with those weaknesses. Implicit in this understanding is the incarnation. In this understanding, human sickness, frailty, limitation, brokenness are affirmed and transformed into health, strength, limitless resources and wholeness. This is perhaps alluded to in II Corinthians 12:9,

> My Grace is sufficient for you, for my power is
> made perfect in weakness. I will all the more
> boast of my weakness, that the power of Christ
> may rest upon me.

In Eucharistic celebrations, christians, and especially the sick, are called upon to bring their afflictions and anxieties to Christ. There is no guarantee of instant solution, or a problem-free life. But in every situation, God's grace is available to enable them to cope. So those who are sick and afflicted can come with gratitude and hope. They can say with the writer of Romans,

> If God is for us, who is against us? Who shall
> bring charge to God's elect? Who shall separate
> us from the love of Christ? Shall tribulation or
> distress, or persecution or famine, peril? No,

in all things we are more than conquerors through
Him who loved us.
(Rms. 8:31, 33, 35, 37)

The Eucharist for christians who are sick can also be <u>ker-</u>

<u>ygmatic</u>, a celebration of the work of God.

It is a great thanksgiving to God, for everything
accomplished in creation, redemption and sancti-
fication, for everything accomplished by God now
in the church and in the world in spite of the
sins of human beings, for everything that God
will accomplish in bringing the kingdom to fulfillment.[21]

In interpreting this ritual as communion, the notion

of fellowship is emphasized. It calls for regrouping of

members of the family/clan for the purpose of reconcilia-

tion. In the fellowship all are called to settle differ-

ences, hurts and hatreds in order to love, make friends and

eat together. It calls for those estranged and isolated to

find company. In times of sickness, one is tempted natu-

rally to recoil and withdraw. In the notion of communion,

christians who are sick are reminded of the community of

Christ where they can claim some sense of belonging. The

African christian who is sick has much in his/her culture

to make this image meaningful and appropriate. Therefore,

the interpretation of the act of communion calls christians

to be one family, with one head, one Lord. Christians

belong to that one family by baptism in the name of God,

the Father; in the name of Jesus, the ancestor and redeem-

er, and in the name of the Holy Spirit. This interpretation will enrich the African notion of collective identity and the implied christian sense of <u>Koinonia</u>.

The name, "the Lord's Supper", focuses on the act of eating, the celebration, the banquet meal. It is seen as a continuation of the feeding of the five thousand or echoing the same theological significance of the wedding at Cana where Jesus performed the first miracle. The new element here is the instruction to remember. The disciples are called upon to remember Jesus' sacrifice for them. His death was a sacrifice to absorb guilt, to draw humanity close to God and to each other. Here, the eating symbolically represents the narrowing of the gap, emphasizing the sense of oneness.

All are united to the maker and to each other. In the eating of the bread and drinking of the wine, God's will is accepted for reconciliation and for responsibility to work out problems. Christians are sent on an arduous mission characterized by the life of Christ, their first ancestor. Christians become agents of the good news. By eating together, christians seal their sense of belonging with their creator and with each other.

This is one of the metaphors that can catch the vivid imagination of Africans in general and expresses a christological truth which has parallels in the traditions of various communities in Africa. The place for sacrificial meals as part of a total package of healing is an important if not an indispensable one. Therefore, to tell the sick that God has offered Himself to forgive them their sins, wrongs, failures in Christ, is good news. It removes the burden of guilt and fear or anxiety for being punished. In this meal of Christ, the broken relationships are restored; the bond of all humanity is reestablished in Christ. The Christ event interpreted as a meal also implies that christians who participate in it share a new value system where all are neighbours, brothers and sisters, mothers and fathers. The bond of the extended family is strengthened. This bond includes the Saints who have gone before them, Africans might say one's ancestors and the first ancestor, Christ. The sick can then say with joy and relief that He took their infirmities and bore their diseases (Matt. 8:-17). Therefore, the sick pledge with the rest of the christian community, mutual amity and dependence. Indeed in the traditional societies, one only eats sacred meals with members of the same family or clan; one does not eat them with strangers. So, in the Banquet of Jesus Christ is celebrated the salvation of mind, body and soul of the community. Peace and harmony are restored in the community. Perhaps, this is what the minister alludes to when he uses the words, "The body of our Lord Jesus Christ which was given for you, to preserve your body and soul into everlasting life."[22]

The sacrificial meal emphasis on this rite for the christians in Africa with their cultural background will help them "reach down into the well spring of their faith and discover peace and serenity (forgiveness and reconciliation) in the face of pain and suffering."[23]

This may not be the end for some christians. In some cases, the relatives of the sick and some of the 'accused' may not be christians. This raises a complex christological question which has never been adequately nor boldly faced by the church in Africa. Does the church admit all members of the family of a christian who is sick into the Lord's Supper for the purpose of reconciliation and healing for that person? Is the Lord's Supper an internal part of the word of God to all humanity? Is it open to all? Why or why not? If communion is a means of grace, as some Reformers especially Presbyterians believe, then why prevent the "sinners" this means of grace? As Jesus said, He came for sinners. These questions are crucial when the sick person has a spouse who is not a christian. Has the advice of the writer of first Corinthians, that "the unbelieving husband is consecrated through his wife [believing wife] and the unbelieving wife is consecrated through her husband" (1 Corinth. 7:14) any contribution to make to these questions? Even though this text is specifically related to the issue of divorce, one is tempted to suggest that it can be expanded to all aspects of the marriage

relationship, in divorce or not, in sickness and good
health. There are many responses to these questions and
this pastoral problem in Africa. One such approach is
pursued by Masamba Ma Mpolo. He seems to suggest that the
traditional sacraments and those of the christian tradition
should go side by side as their purposes have the same
goal. He argues that,

> the sacramental dimensions of the symbolic con-
> nects those individuals to the ultimate truth of
> life and assures them the reality of their con-
> tinuity as part of the extended family, helping
> individuals to establish an equilibrium between
> one's self and social self.[24]

This type of approach may well be a casuistric approach
rather than a general principle of pastoral care. It would
be better to integrate some of these symbols rather than
offer dualistic models of christian theology of pastoral
care versus traditional methods of care concurrently.

As indicated earlier, the model offered in this thesis
is one of integration. This is how one might attempt to
answer the questions raised. The celebration in the Lord's
Supper should be followed by a peace meal. In this meal,
all those connected with the sick person, either as accused
directly or indirectly or as care givers, must be invited,
for sickness is one of those forces that disturbs the in-
trapersonal and interpersonal stability and solidarity.
Theologically, it is a practical application of the One
Reconciliation in Christ. It is an appropriation of that

reconciliation in a particular case that involves all. It is following the example of the Samaritan woman at the well (John 4:7-30). She received reconciliation from Jesus and became a reconciler herself. She was no longer a mean, condemned sinner, but a saint who announced to her people to come for reconciliation. In that peace meal, reconciliation is there announced to all; the sick announce it by their presence and words, prayer, or other form. Those concerned directly or indirectly can come forward for confession, and acceptance; then forgiveness is granted to all by all. In other words, whatever is done in the society, whatever symbols are appropriated and reappropriated, all issue from the One Reconciliation in Jesus Christ and revolve around that. The model advocated here is a dialectical dialogue. This approach will eliminate the old missionary model of separating people from their families in the name of christianity. The dialectical dialogue model echoes the spirit of unity expressed in Jesus' prayer in John 17.

For the purpose of pastoral care for the christians who are sick, these different emphases are alternatives to use when and if appropriate. They call christian diviners in Africa to develop a high degree of sensitivity to where their members are spiritually, psychologically and sociologically. They call for a deeper awareness of the cultural and particular family milieu of the member who is sick.

As indicated earlier, denominationalism is important but its importance is secondary when pastoral needs of a member call for a different model of interpretation or presentation of the christian resources. There is no need for blindly following divisions that missionaries imported, divisions which do not have any immediate relevance to the situation of church members and do not meet their pastoral needs especially in times of sickness.

125

Footnotes

[1]Don Browning (ed.), *Practical Theology* (San Francisco: Harper and Row Publishers, 1980, p. 169.

[2]Seward Hiltner, *Preface to Pastoral Theology* (Nashville: Abingdon Press, 1985), p. 22.

[3]*Ibid.*

[4]William A. Clebsch and Charles R. Jaekle, *Pastoral Care in Historical Perspective* (Englewood Cliffs, New Jersey: Prentice-Hall, 1964), p. 76.

[5]Masamba Ma Mpolo, "African Symbols and Stories in Pastoral Care", *Journal of Pastoral Care*, 39 (1985): 322.

[6]*Ibid.*

[7]Benjamin Ray, *African Religions: Symbols, Rituals and Community* (Englewood Cliffs, New Jersey: Prentice-Hall Inc., 1976), p. 104.

[8]Richard E. Palmer, *Hemeneutics* (Evanston: Northwestern University Press, 1969), p. 13.

[9]Dr. Richard Yadeau, "Healing", *World and War*, 11(4) (Fall 1982): 319.

[10]Charles Gerkin, "Revisioning Pastoral Counselling in a Hermeneutic Mode", *The Living Human Document* (Nashville: Abingdon Press, 1984), p. 26.

[11]*Ibid.*, p. 27.

[12]Morris Maddock, *The Christian Healing Ministry* (London: SPCK, 1981), p. 58-59.

[13]*Ibid.*

[14]Alyward Shorter, *Jesus and the Witch Doctors: An Approach to Healing and Wholeness* (New York: Orbis Books, 1985), p. 11.

[15]Joseph Martos, *Doors to the Sacred* (New York: Image Books, 1982), p. 16.

[16]John Calvin, Institutes of Christian Religion, trans. Henry Beveridge (Grand Rapids: William B. Eerdmans Publishing Co., 1964), IV, XIV3.

[17]Ibid., IV, XIV7.

[18]Ibid., IV XIII9.

[19]G.C. Berkouwer, "Institutes of Religion: Studies in Dogmatics", The Sacraments (Grand Rapids: William B. Eerdmans Publisher, 1969).

[20]Robert C. Broderick, The Catholic Encyclopedia (Nashville: Thomas Nelson Publishers, 1976), p. 375-376.

[21]Baptism, Eucharist and Ministry, Faith and Order Paper No. 111, Geneva, WCC, 1982, p. 10.

[22]Brian A. Brown, The Sacramental Ministry to the Sick (New York: Exposition Press, 1969), p. 58.

[23]George R. Robie and Edmund Klimek, "Ministry to Those Who are Sick", Pastoral Life 35(1) (Jan. 1986): 26.

[24]Mosamba Ma Mpolo, "African Symbols and Stories in Pastoral Care", Journal of Pastoral Care, p. 325.

6. SUMMARY AND CONCLUSION

For Africans, a human being is not said to be alive
and healthy because the mechanisms of the human anatomy are
functioning well. It is not just the absence of bacteria,
germs or diseases. Life for Africans is a harmony of the
individual and the whole of nature. Life for Africans is
an encounter with the sacred every moment.

Life is sacramental, so when life is out of order then
sacramental means must be deployed in order to bring life
back into harmony with all of creation. This involves all
the agents associated, or perceived to be sacred and connected, in the well being of the individual. All the
forces that protect the individual must be reactivated,
charged or reconnected with the various energy sources in
the spiritual realm, in social relationships and in the
community as a whole. One is restored or reconnected
through the everyday rituals such as eating, drinking and
washing.

Christian theology of pastoral care to the christians
who are sick has been integrated with African culture in
order to be meaningful and relevant. It is therefore imperative that christian theology has sought to relate to
the place of Africans on earth, and even more specifically,
to the place of the individual(s) in the rest of the community. The author has tried to help christians who are

sick draw upon their christian faith, which expresses itself through the images and actions in which the crisis of
meaning expresses itself.

In most cases, the feelings of African christians who
are sick consist of guilt, alienation and despair. These
feelings, if not attended to, are enough to spark off psychosomatic illness or to increase an already existing sickness. Sickness in the African concept also implies seeking
for what Paul Tillich calls the "ground of being" or the
ultimate reality or meaning of existence. For "to live" in
Africa means "to participate in". If and when one cannot
participate in, then the ultimate quests for meaning are
raised. The church, in this case, is called upon to make
its message of forgiveness meaningful.

The Judeo-christian faith has been made to proclaim
God as one whose interest is to share in the daily tribula-
tions of people in order to enable them to cope with their
problems. The word of God has spoken of God as one who
became a human and dwelt among humans. Therefore, the
author has tried to show that the christian church in Africa can no longer limit itself to preaching exclusively
about God and the world. This kind of preaching of what
God can do, or will do, is not sufficient for those christians who are sick. For African christians who are sick,
they no longer worry as much about what is outside them as
they do about what is inside of them. In this thesis, they

must be made to feel and experience God who can help them stand their ground against the invasion of evil forces. They can count on an inner faith which can be channeled into a total personality, actively engaged with the environment.

One is tempted to suggest or even predict that if the christian church cannot be counted upon to reach the African christian in sickness, then christianity will lose its potency, relevance and impact. For who needs a faith that only rejoices and celebrates but which cannot be counted upon in times of weeping and mourning? The author has attempted to respond to that challenge of the christian ministry of healing. He has attempted to respond to the African christians' search for survival, meaning and forgiveness in times of sickness.

Among other things, the author has attempted a rediscovering of the full orbit of christian symbols and rituals. One cannot but echo the words of Samuel Miller, which summarize the intent of this thesis beautifully. He writes:

> Symbols in their constantly changing power and expressions can make the christian church and its ministers aware that human life is never as flat and black and white as rational theological concepts and words imply. The depth, mystery and fertility of religious experience and liturgical expression should refresh and reform the life of the church lest it become a petrifact of a once vital faith.[1]

The prophetic words of Samuel Miller are no more true anywhere than in Africa for two reasons. Firstly, the use of
symbol and rituals in African culture makes it imperative
for christian theology to look for ways of integrating the
African symbols and rituals. Secondly, the church is en-
joying an enviable, adolescent stage with vigor and admira-
tion. However, if the church does not take roots by integration, the collapse and almost total disappearance of
christianity in North Africa can be experienced in Ghana
once more in history.

This author has attempted to show that culture provides a great opportunity for a christian theology of pastoral care to the sick. Implicit in this task is the fact
that in our common humanity, humans are humans, pain is
pain, love is love everywhere. What is different is the
means by which we can perceive and interpret our world of
meanings. If christians can take some of these differences
as gifts of God together with our commonness, we will make
it possible for all of God's creation, in Europe, Asia,
North America as well as Africa, to hear, touch, smell,
feel, see or experience the unconditional love of God in
Christ which calls us together into a community of love and
hope.

Footnotes

[1]Hans Hofmann (ed.), *Making the Ministry Relevant* (New York: Charles Scribner's Sons, 1960), p. xi.

Bibliography

Appiah-Kubi, Kofi. Man Cures, God Heals. New York:
Friendship Press, 1981.

Appiah-Kubi, Kofi and Tories, Virginia. African Theology
En Route. New York: Orbis Books, 1979.

Bakan, David. Disease, Pain and Sacrifice. Chicago:
University of Chicago, 1981.

Baptism, Eucharist and Ministry, Faith and Order Paper,
No. 111, Geneva, W.C.C., 1982.

Berkouwer, G.C. Studies in Dogmatics: The Sacraments.
Grand Rapids: William B. Eerdman Publishers, 1969.

Broderick, Robert C. The Catholic Encyclopedia. Nashville: Thomas Nelson Publishers, 1976.

Brown, Brian A. The Sacramental Ministry to the Sick.
New York: Exposition Press, 1969.

Browning, C., ed. Practical Theology. San Francisco:
Harper and Row, 1980.

Calvin, John. Institutes of Christian Religion. Trans.
Henry Beveridge. Grand Rapids: William B. Eerdman
Publishers, 1964.

Clebsch, William A. and Jaekle, Charles R. Pastoral
Care in Historical Perspective. New Jersey:
Prentice-Hall, 1964.

Clinebell, Howard. Basic Types of Pastoral Counselling.
Nashville: Abingdon Press, 1982.

Cochrane, Charles Norris. Christianity and Classical
Culture. New York: Oxford University Press, 1944.

Dickson, Kwesi. Theology in Africa. New York: Orbis
Books, 1984.

Field, M.J. Religion and Medicine of the Ga People.
London: Oxford University Press, 1937.

Fortes, Meyer. The Dynamics of Clanship Among the
Tallensis. London: Oxford University Press, 1945.

Fortes, Meyer. The Web of Kinship Among the Tallensis. London: Oxford University Press, 1949.

Geertz, Clifford. The Interpretation of Cultures. New York: Basic Books, 1973.

Gerkin, Charles V. The Living Human Document. Nashville: Abingdon Press, 1958.

Hiltner, Seward. Preface to Pastoral Theology. Nashville: Abingdon Press, 1958.

Hogan, Robert. Personality Theory: Personology Tradition. New Jersey: Prentice-Hall, 1979.

Hofmann, Hans (ed.). Making Ministry Relevant. New York: Charles Scribner's Sons, 1960.

Holifield, Brooks E. A History of Pastoral Care in America: Salvation to Self Realization. Nashville: Abingdon Press, 1985.

In Disciplinary Decrees of the General Council. The Fourth Lateran Council Cannons 21-11. Translation and commentary by Schroeder. St. Louis: B. Herider book Co., 1937.

Johnson, Paul E. Psychology of Pastoral Care: The Pastoral Ministry in Theory and Practice. Nashville: Abingdon Press, 1953.

Jung, C.G. Two Essays on Analytical Psychology. New York: Orbis Books, 1981.

Lake, Frank. Clinical Theology. London: Dorton, Longman and Todd, 1966.

Lambourne, R.A. Community, Church, and Healing: A Study of Some Corporate Aspects of the Church's Ministry to the Sick. London: Dorton, Longman and Todd, 1963.

Mackenzie, John. Souls in the Making: Introduction to Pastoral Psychology. New York: Macmillan, 1929.

Maddock, Morris. The Christian Healing Ministry. London: SPCK, 1981.

Marshall, Nathaneal. The Pennitential Discipline of the Primitive Church. London: 1714, Oxford University, 1944.

Martos, Joseph. Doors to the Sacred. New York: Image Books, 1982.

Marty, Martin E. "Large Confession". Health and Medicine in the Lutheran Tradition. Crossword, NY 1983.

Mbiti, John. New Testament Eschatology in African Background. London: Oxford University Press, 1971.

McNeil, John T. A History of the Care of Souls. New York: Harper and Row Publishers, 1951.

Niebuhr, H. Richard and William, David D., eds. The Ministry in Historical Perspective. New York: Harper and Row, 1956.

Oates, Wayne. New Dimension in Pastoral Care. Philadelphia Fortress Press, 1970.

Palmer, Richard R. Hermeneutics. Evanston: Northwestern University Press, 1969.

Pobee, John S. Toward An African Theology. Nashville: Abingdon Press, 1979.

Ray, Benjamin. African Religions: Symbols, Rituals and Community. Englewood Cliffs, New Jersey: Prentice-Hall Inc., 1976.

Schleiermacher, Friederich. Brief Outline on the Study of Theology. Translated by Torrence N. Tice. Richmond: John Knox, 1966.

Schreiter, Robert. Constructing Local Theologies. New York: Orbis books, 1981.

Shorter, Alyward. Jesus and the Witch Doctor: An Approach to Healing as Wholeness. New York: Orbis Books, 1985.

Shorter, Alyward. African Culture and the Christian Church. New York: Orbis Books, 1974.

Sow, Ibrahim. Anthropological Structures of Madness in Black Africa. Englewood Cliffs, New Jersey: Prentice-Hall Inc., 1976.

Sundkler, B.G.M. Bantu Prophets in South Africa. London: Oxford University Press, 1961.

Thayer, Nelson T. Spirituality and Pastoral Care.
Philadelphia: Fortress Press, 1985.

"The Corrector of Burchard Worms". Medieval Handbook
of Pennance. Translated by John McNeil and Helena
M. Gamer. New York: Columbia University, 1938.

Tillich, Paul. Courage To Be. New Haven: Yale
University Press, 1952.

Tournier, Paul. Four Best Books in One Volume. New
York: Iverson-Norman, 1977.

Van Oosterzee, J.J. Practical Theology. New York:
Scribner Sons, 1898.

Willston, Walker. A History of the Christian Church.
Revised by C.C. Richardson, W. Panck and R.T. Handy.
New York: Charles Scribner and Sons, 1959.

Wise, Carrol. The Meaning of Pastoral Care. New York:
Harper and Row Publishers, 1966.

136

Periodicals

Evans-Pritchard. "The Meaning of Sacrifice Among the
Neurs". Journal of the Royal Anthropological
Society 84, 1954.

Foster, George M. "Disease Etiologies in Non Western
Medical Systems". American Anthropologist 78,
1976.

Kravetz, Howard M. "Illness and Religion: A Physician's
Testimony". Journal of Pastoral Care 12, 1958.

Ma Mpolo, Masamba. "African Symbols and Stories".
Journal of Pastoral Care 39, 1985.

Mehl, Roger. "The Biblical Understanding of Community
and Person". Canadian Journal of Theology 5 & 6,
1959-1960.

Mendosa, Eugene L. "The Soul and Sacrifices Among the
Sisala". Journal of Religion in Africa 8 (date
unknown) Fase 1.

Oden, Thomas. "Rediscovering Lost Identity". Journal
of Pastoral Care 4(5), March 1980.

Robie, George R. and Klimek, Edmund. "Ministry to Those
Who are Sick". Pastoral Life 35(1), January 1985.

Seijas, H. "An Approach to the Study of the Medical
Aspects of Culture". Current Anthropology, December,
1973.

Simundson, Daniel J. "The Healing Church and Its
Ministry". Word and World 2(4), Fall 1982.

Yadeau, Richard E. "Healing". Word and World 2(5), Fall
1982.

Abraham Adu Berinyuu, minister of the Presbyterian Church of Ghana, previously tutor at the Ecumenical Training Centre, Tamale, Ghana. Graduate of Trinity College, Legon, Ghana; Knox College, University of Toronto; Atlantic School of Theology, Halifax, Nova Scotia.

This book resulted from my pastoral work with both city and rural congregations and my own background of being born and raised in a rural situation, coupled with my training in Clinical Pastoral Education in the Hospital for Sick Children, Toronto; Toronto Western Hospital, and the Nova Scotia Psychiatric Hospital, Datmouth.

Presently a Ph.D. candidate in Pastoral Theology at the Princeton Theological Seminary.

STUDIEN ZUR INTERKULTURELLEN GESCHICHTE DES CHRISTENTUMS
ETUDES D'HISTOIRE INTERCULTURELLE DU CHRISTIANISME
STUDIES IN THE INTERCULTURAL HISTORY OF CHRISTIANITY

Begründet von/fondé par/founded by
Hans Jochen Margull †, Hamburg

Herausgegeben von/edité par/edited by

Richard Friedli   Walter J. Hollenweger   Theo Sundemeier
Université de Fribourg   University of Birmingham   Universität Heidelberg

Jan A.B. Jongeneel
Rijksuniversiteit Utrecht

Band   1   Wolfram Weiße: Südafrika und das Antirassismusprogramm. Kirchen im Spannungsfeld einer Rassengesellschaft.

Band   2   Ingo Lembke: Christentum unter den Bedingungen Lateinamerikas. Die katholische Kirche vor den Problemen der Abhängigkeit und Unterentwicklung.

Band   3   Gerd Uwe Kliewer: Das neue Volk der Pfingstler. Religion, Unterentwicklung und sozialer Wandel in Lateinamerika.

Band   4   Joachim Wietzke: Theologie im modernen Indien - Paul David Devanandan.

Band   5   Werner Ustorf: Afrikanische Initiative. Das aktive Leiden des Propheten Simon Kimbangu.

Band   6   Erhard Kamphausen: Anfänge der kirchlichen Unabhängigkeitsbewegung in Südafrika. Geschichte und Theologie der äthiopischen Bewegung. 1880-1910.

Band   7   Lothar Engel: Kolonialismus und Nationalismus im deutschen Protestantismus in Namibia 1907-1945. Beiträge zur Geschichte der deutschen evangelischen Mission und Kirche im ehemaligen Kolonial- und Mandatsgebiet Südwestafrika.

Band   8   Pamela M. Binyon: The Concepts of "Spirit" and "Demon". A Study in the use of different languages describing the same phenomena.

Band   9   Neville Richardson: The World Council of Churches and Race Relations. 1960 to 1969.

Band 10   Jörg Müller: Uppsala II. Erneuerung in der Mission. Eine redaktionsgeschichtliche Studie und Dokumentation zu Sektion II der 4. Vollversammlung des Ökumenischen Rates der Kirchen, Uppsala 1968.

Band 11   Hans Schöpfer: Theologie und Gesellschaft. Interdisziplinäre Grundlagenbibliographie zur Einführung in die befreiungs- und polittheologische Problematik: 1960-1975.

Band 12   Werner Hoerschelmann: Christliche Gurus. Darstellung von Selbstverständnis und Funktion indigenen Christseins durch unabhängige charismatisch geführte Gruppen in Südindien.

Band 13   Claude Schaller: L'Eglise en quéte de dialogue. Vergriffen.

Band 14   Theo Tschuy: Hundert Jahre kubanischer Protestantismus (1868-1961). Versuch einer kirchengeschichtlichen Darstellung.

Band 15   Werner Korte: Wir sind die Kirchen der unteren Klassen. Entstehung, Organisation und gesellschaftliche Funktionen unabhängiger Kirchen in Afrika.

Band 16   Arnold Bittlinger: Pabst und Pfingstler. Der römisch katholisch-pfingstliche Dialog und seine ökumenische Relevanz.

Band 17   Ingemar Lindén: The Last Trump. An historico-genetical study of some important chapters in the making and development of the Seventh-day Adventist Church.

Band 18   Zwinglio Dias: Krisen und Aufgaben im brasilianischen Protestantismus. Eine Studie zu den sozialgeschichtlichen Bedingungen und volkspädagogischen Möglichkeiten der Evangelisation.

Band 19   Mary Hall: A quest for the liberated Christian, Examined on the basis of a mission, a man and a movement as agents of liberation.

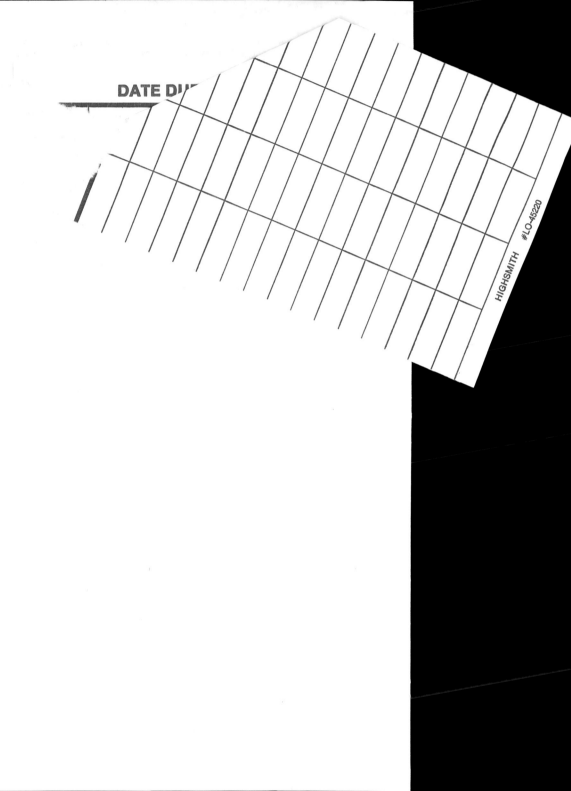

DATE DUE